For alcoholic beverages, without which this book would be very boring.

A note from me

Everyone has avoided adulthood at some stage in their life. You have, I have, your mum has. Some people do this at the weekend, they clock out of work and let their hair down. Others sit and play the PlayStation for an evening or watch something funny on Netflix. I know people who have taken 30-minute loo breaks to avoid adult life, they called it 'paid to poo.' Adulthood is pretty scary. There is no set age limit for when you reach it but at some stage, you'll have things to do other than just waking up and existing. Bills, jobs, kids, making small talk with people, it all of a sudden just hits you and that's it, you're an adult.

I avoided adulthood for a whole year in 2017 which resulted eventually in this book. It is a book that I've loved writing and my family have hated proofreading. They thought my travels consisted of temples and lovely scenery when the truth is it consisted of cheap beer and hangovers. I wanted to write something a bit different than the usual travel book/blog and let you know what happens when someone sneaks off somewhere for a year or two. Of course, some people do jet off and find themselves whilst meditating with a Buddhist monk but I've assumed you don't want to hear about that. If you do want to hear about that just find someone with a pair of genie pants on, they will tell you *all* about their gap year.

Is this going to be the best book you've ever read? I doubt it! You'll find punctuation errors, spelling mistakes and I'm sure some sentences won't even make sense. I wasn't about to shell out for a proofreader. Don't worry about that, it's not a dissertation. If it will make you feel better to red ink the errors and give me a mark out of 100 please do so but I've done three drafts and I'm Ian Bealed, I've got nothing left.

After reading this book my mum told me I needed to grow up and I told her I was avoiding that then. I guess you could say I was avoiding adulthood. Please don't shut the book, it gets better than that. But it made her laugh and that's the main reason I wrote this book, to make people laugh. That and being furloughed was exceptionally boring. Get yourself in your most immature mindset and enjoy! Please don't take this book or yourself too seriously and may you laugh to yourself at least once.

Introduction

Alright? My name is Harry Boucher and I was and still am afraid to grow up. This is the story of my travels back in 2017 when I was a bright-eyed and clueless 22-year-old with absolutely nothing to lose. I hope you'll be glad to know I'm not the typical 'rah' daddies money traveller, if not this is going to be a long book for you. You won't find any inspirational quotes here, unless you are inspired by moaning and drunkenness. If you are looking to read about how someone found their soul and cleansed their sins whilst indulging in culture, please close this book immediately. I am not here to give you travel tips, I very much doubt this book will be the shove you need to quit your job, put your life on your back and bugger off somewhere abroad that isn't Gran Canaria or Turkey. That said, if you hate your job and don't have much to lose, stop moping about the place bringing everyone else down and go and see some of the world! If for some reason reading this does become persuasive please do not leave your good job, partner and kids behind and sneak over to Thailand, that will not go down well.

I was a crap traveller, unorganised to the extreme and I spent way too much time in places I shouldn't have and money on things I didn't need like buckets of vodka and offensive vests that exposed my nipples. Those who have travelled might have liked places that I found to be average and they are entitled to their wrong opinion. If I've described your favourite travelling spot as a steaming pile of dung please don't be offended, we are all different. For example, some blokes think dreadlocks look cool, can you imagine?!

Yeovil in sunny Somerset is my birthplace and current home. I'm not a farmer but I am a bit 'ooh arrr'. I will explain any strange lingo used as best as I can throughout the book as I know people from other areas struggle to understand certain sayings. You will hear a lot about Ben Cheveralls (Chevs) and Callum Tyrie (Tyrie) throughout this book, creative nicknames I know. They are from Essex so they speak a bit like those TOWIE idiots from the tele only they have three brain cells instead of the usual one that is frequently issued in that area of the UK.

So, a bit of background of how I ended up going travelling. The period of my life between September 2015 and December 2016 was a seemingly never-ending shower of shit. My dream job as a motoring journalist ended in October 2015, let's say by mutual consent, my performance was described as unsatisfactory which was very true but I did hate the work. All of a sudden, I needed work as I had rent to pay on my flat in Southampton which is how I ended up at ParcelForce as a delivery driver for the festive period. This lasted for a total of two weeks. I crashed a van right in front of the area manager, sideswiped another van and the damage was substantial. That'll do it. I can vividly remember sitting in my car after getting sacked from ParcelForce and thinking how shit my life was. I was lower than a snake's belly.

I had six months left on my flat, so I needed to get another job as soon as possible. Searching the job boards, it became apparent that I was either going to be a wanky salesman shouting at old ladies in the high street, a waiter or a carer. I went for an interview in a sales team and I have never met a more horrid set of people in my life. Everyone was standing up with headsets on shouting like they were working on Wall Street. They were selling insurance. No thanks. I didn't fancy being a waiter either so in January 2016 I started my career as a carer. This involved but was not limited too making cups of tea and chatting with old people which I enjoyed hugely by the way.

Fast forward six months and I was at the end of the lease on the flat in Southampton. Chevs had lived with me through university and then in the flat for the year afterwards. We went to Solent University, so we are thicker than the University of Southampton students, but we do have a personality. He worked in a pub and gave me good discounts on food and booze, all in all, he was a top flatmate and is a great friend. It was on a hungover Sunday with Tyrie down to visit that the fateful question was floated in the room. 'Fancy going travelling?'

We all evaluated our lives in the following seconds and realised we had absolutely nothing to lose, on reflection, it was quite sad. Tyrie served pints to the posh at a golf club in Essex, Chevs served pints to rough geezers in Southampton and I chatted about the soaps to those in need across the Hampshire region. You know what, travelling sounds like a good plan! I thought this process would've taken a few weeks to decide, some consulting on the locations we wanted to visit, asking a few friends who have been already, maybe a glance at TripAdvisor. It didn't. The next day Tyrie and I went into STA Travel and booked it, a one-way flight to Bangkok, please.

We all decided on January 2017 as a departure date as we would all need to save some money. During my four years in Southampton, I was somewhere in the region of £6,000 down. That's not counting the 40 grands worth of debt I was and am still in for a Sports Journalism degree that's as useful as Anne Frank's drum kit. I needed a change in lifestyle so I ended up back in Somerset, sponging off mum and dad for six months and saying yes to every single care shift on offer. I even worked Christmas Day and between you and me, I was extremely hungover and had to be silent-sick in a customer's bathroom.

Nothing else mattered any more, not my pointless degree in writing about sport, not my van crash and not my slightly larger than I'd like waistline. I was off travelling with two of my best mates. After a massive piss up in Essex.

Disclaimer: Below is a photo of me, in it I have zero hair. This is because I am a closet bald man that wears a glue-on wig nowadays. Bradley Wiggins / Wig Narstie / Wiggy Azalea has been on my head for a year or so now and I didn't have this life-changing option before travelling as I was extremely poor. I also can't remember the names of everyone that I met so I am just going to name them randomly, probably after characters on the Netflix show I have been watching that day. I will also convert everything into pounds when possible to make everything more relatable, saves you Googling 'Thai Baht to GBP' to work out how much I paid for a toastie and a pint.

Just so you know the state of the trio of idiots who left for
Thailand back in 2017, here's a photo of us at our leaving beers.

Callum Tyrie, me & Ben Cheveralls

Thailand

Thursday 12th January 2017

I made a genuinely awful video of me packing my backpack to put on Instagram, was I already an annoying traveller before I had even left the country? It was sped up and had some funky music in the background and I received a large barrage of abuse from my mates for making it which was completely understandable. How was anyone supposed to know I was going travelling if I didn't post it all over social media? Once I was packed it was time to head to Heathrow and meet Chevs and Tyrie. Only mum and dad came to see me off, my younger sisters weren't arsed at all. Poppy, my youngest sister, was getting my bedroom so if anything, she was excited. It's quite a nice scene in the airport seeing families wave off their loved ones. Tyrie's mum cried waving her youngest son off, Chevs's mum did too. My mum was a little emotional, but my old man was as chirpy as I have ever seen him, some might describe him as happy that I was departing. He's only ever smiled in two pictures; one is with Paddy Madden after Yeovil gained promotion to the Championship and the other is with me leaving the country. In fairness to him, he was going to have an extra Yorkshire Pudding on a Sunday now. After quick walkthrough security and checking our bags in the first leg of our journey was underway. First stop, the airport pub for an overpriced pint.

On the plane to Mumbai, I took the first of my Malaria tablets as there was going to be one or two mosquitos in South East Asia if the rumours were correct. I had spent a small fortune on a load of these tablets, so I was hoping to see at least one flying malaria carrier. Five minutes after taking the first tablet I started to feel strange. Side effects of these tablets were known to be; shitting your insides out, puking your lungs out through your nose and tripping balls (hallucinating). We were only about 20 minutes from our Mumbai Airport change so I would soon find out which side effect I was going to have. Would I birth my insides via my backside, or would I think the toilet was a race-car?

Sadly, for me, it was not the latter and my entire insides including the awful curry I had just consumed on the plane fell out of me. It was without question the most unpleasant numero two I have ever taken. The toilet was just a tiled hole in the ground and the toilet paper was not anywhere near substantial enough. Somehow, I had to sort myself out and get on another plane to Bangkok. If I'd have shit myself on the plane I would've immediately returned home. Tyrie had no side effects from his tablets and Chevs hadn't bought any. Chevs would rather spend his money on beers than he would potentially live-saving tablets. He wasn't going to be sat on the plane from Mumbai to Bangkok with his backside clenched for the entire journey so who was the real winner? Well, me if we got bitten, but at that moment, Chevs was winning 1-0.

I somehow made it to Bangkok without watery poo running down my leg. The excitement had taken over and I had forgotten that I had taken a cross between MDMA and a Laxative. This was what I had been looking forward to for months. Freedom, cheap beers, partying, buckets of booze, sun. Culture and stuff too but mainly carefree boozing and tanning. But first, and most importantly, bed. It was a seriously long day of travelling and as much as I'd like to come across as a super-cool party animal, I was tired and I needed my full eight hours kip. Luckily Tyrie had sorted us out with a hostel miles away from backpacker central in Bangkok. Imagine going for a weekend in central London but staying in Surrey. A truly awful location but I was thankful for his incompetence, it was quiet and I slept like a baby.

Saturday 14th January 2017

I had nothing to say to Tyrie about our first stop. It was a place called Silom and it was as lively as an end-of-life ward in a hospital. The hostel we slept in was only for one night and was fully booked that night so we couldn't stay there again. This was our big opportunity to get in a taxi to Khao San Road (backpacker central) but instead, we found a hotel in Silom and give it a chance to get livelier at night. The hotel was expensive and nice, but I'm not interested in nice, this wasn't Travels With My Father. I wanted to be in a 12-bed dorm with Germans drinking from a funnel and playing stupid drinking games. Either way, one thing we were certainly doing on our first day of travelling was having a beer or 16. The beer was expensive here and the bars were very quiet. We all discussed and agreed that Silom was crap and we needed to be leaving the next day. With all three of us in agreement, we successfully got super drunk despite it costing us £3 a pint. I know that is a reasonable price for the UK but when you're budgeting for £1 beers or less it is a real kick in the nuts. It never did get lively in Silom, much later in our travels we found out that it was the gay capital of Bangkok which explained why there was an abundance of men wearing short shorts.

Sunday 15th January 2017

Khao San Road, the gateway for travellers across South East Asia. Most people either start or end their travels through South East Asia here. Imagine Magaluf, Ayai Napa or any other budget boozy holiday you have ever been on and times it by eight million. This place was bonkers. Our taxi driver dropped us off at the bottom of the road and looked at us shaking his head and muttering to himself 'silly British boys'. We wandered up the entire street and it was like being on another planet, a place Louis Theroux would visit whilst filming 'The World's Weirdest Places.' That's a show I would binge! It was 10 am and I saw people that were eating breakfast with a cocktail bucket, people who were clearly still on it from the night before and a few people asleep on the pavement who hadn't made it back to their hostel. I also saw my first 'ladyboy' which was quite a moment for me. I'll be perfectly honest, she was stunning and if it wasn't for her grabbing her penis and asking me if 'I likey' I would have never known. I was also offered to buy a few suits, this was a big thing in Bangkok, men hassled people on the streets to buy a suit from them constantly, much like the parasites in the UK trying to sell life insurance to oldies in the supermarket. I admired their tenacity but I had no room in my backpack for a three-piece suit and a couple of shirts.

We stumbled through the madness to the top of the road and found our hostel. It was another Tyrie find and it was suitably crap. We had a three-bed room at the top of this hostel which looked like a graphic from a Call Of Duty map, it was a bomb site. Our room was a large fridge with a big bed in it and that was good enough. We chucked our stuff in the room and power walked to the nearest bar where it was 70 pence for a pint and £3 for a bucket of blackout juice. This was what it was all about! Every single bar was rammed with travellers getting themselves in a right pickle. We did our very best to crawl the strip from top to bottom but only made it about halfway down from what my brain can officially remember.

Monday 16th January 2017

I was pronounced dead at the scene in the room, the reason of death being an extreme hangover from cheap Vodka. I couldn't remember past 8 pm and judging by my texts I was out until just gone 1 am, dangerous that. Just to really kick me whilst I was down, I soon realised that I had lost one of my bank cards which made me want to chop my head off with a blunt axe. A 20 minute, £1.50 a minute phone call to Halifax got it cancelled and ruined my mood even more. There was no sign of Chevs but Tyrie and I were alive in person just not in spirit. Two out of three wasn't a bad effort unless Chevs had died which would have ruined travelling a little. It got to 10:30 am and we decided that it would be a good idea to get some breakfast and fluids in us so we made our way down to the bar in the hostel which was just as awful as the rest of the place.

As we ordered at the bar, I could hear someone struggling to speak behind me, like they were having a severe stroke. This bloke would talk gibberish for a few seconds and then laugh out loud along with another chap. I turned around to see a topless Chevs sitting with a Canadian couple having a beer and seemingly the time of his life. Now is a good time to tell you that Chevs is one of the best drinkers I have ever come across. In his peak, he could do six litres of Frosty Jacks and then go out. Unbelievably, the Canadian chap he was talking to was on a similar level to Chevs, both were spangled.

Tyrie and I mooched over and joined the conversation. 'You getting a fucking beer in or what you pussies?' Mumbled Ben. A three-day bender to start proceedings, fantastic.

Chevs had also got himself two tattoos' somewhere between 6 pm yesterday and breakfast, both just below the bicep and above the elbow crease on either arm. On his right arm, he had the words 'Hello Frances' from one of our favourite films 'Legend' where Tom Hardy plays both the Kray twins. Back in our flat in Southampton, we would watch this film a lot and it made us laugh hysterically. On the other, he had 'here we go 2,3,4.' This is from an old song titled Gordon Is A Moron by Jilted John. We used to play it and sing along before starting pre-drinks at university and getting super drunk. It was, in a strange way, a motivational song for us. Not the best tattoos I've ever seen I'll be honest, but they certainly added character.

Drinks flowed for the whole day and the Canadian couple, Sean and Nicole, were lovely. They were seasoned travellers so gave us many a helpful tip for our journey which had just started. Sean was a loose unit and was up for getting weird, so was Nicole and Ben and after five or so beers so were Tyrie and me. I decided that it would be handy if we started the bar crawl at the bottom of the strip, that way I could see all of the bars that I hadn't made it to the previous night. Chevs made good friends with a local lady-boy that day who was working behind one of the bars, he was in a world of his own. At one stage he, Chevs not the lady-boy, popped off for five minutes and came back wearing the most horrendous pair of genie pants I've ever seen. That night, I ordered a bucket of vodka and coke and it came over as a bottle of vodka in a bucket of ice with a jug of coke. That was enough to send me on the train to pissed central. We zig-zagged up the strip drinking and dancing awfully as we did. Khao San Road was living up to its reputation as a mental institution disguised as a strip of bars.

Tuesday 17th January 2017

The hangover was more bearable however, I was absolutely off my tits on malaria tablets. They had started playing with my head, the walls were closing in on me and they were multi-coloured. A cold shower, there was no hot water that wasn't my choice, and a load of water later I was feeling human again. Chevs being the animal that he was ordered a beer at breakfast and I could only look at him in admiration and say a prayer for his liver. Chevs, Sean and I were going to get some tattoos after drunken discussions the night before. Chevs wanted an elephant on his back because he likes them. Sean wanted a nautical star because he's a basic bitch and I needed to get the correct date of my surgery on my body somewhere, so I agreed to get one as well. Long story short, I have a tattoo on my chest that states the wrong date of my heart surgery. I was a day out, it was on the 2nd September 2009 and I have the 3rd September 2009 tattooed on my chest. Of course, I could just lie about it for the rest of my life, but it drives my slightly autistic brain mad.

A few hours and six Chevs beers later we were in the tattoo parlour and ready to get inked by a man with a Harry Potter lightning bolt scar tattooed on his cheek. Mine was only a small tattoo to be inked just under my left elbow crease. I wanted the tattoo to be thinner, but it is thick and bold, much like myself at that stage of my life. It isn't the best tattoo I have on my body but it is correct. Chevs's elephant was a good tattoo to be fair and I liked Sean's nautical star. It's a tattoo that you can get away with if you have travelled as much as he has, if I had got it after a week in Thailand, I would be nothing less than a massive bell-end. We followed the tattoos with some food and some more beers when Sean asked a peculiar question. 'Have you ever been to a Ping Pong show?'

I would advise against Googling 'Bangkok Ping Pong Show.' If you do you will see women popping ping pong balls out of their lady gardens and other very strange things. If you Google it after reading about this show you're a weirdo. I was slightly naïve, although I had heard about these shows I assumed they would be more like a fun circus than a sex show. I was wrong, so badly wrong. It was like if

American Horror Story made a sex show episode. Things were going inside and coming out of all kinds of orifices that I never thought possible. Creepy men sat in the front row rubbing their thighs and grunting away whilst their wives thought they were on a business trip. Some of it was quite funny, if you don't laugh at a woman blowing out a candle with a fanny-flutter then you have no sense of humour at all. The rest of it was disturbing and we called it a night when a woman popped out the 11th ping pong ball in a row. She might still be going now for all I know.

You know where the night ends up, so I won't bore you with another bucket of booze story. Chevs did manage to squeeze in another tattoo, getting 'Hakuna Matata' tattooed on his chest. I've always thought he should've got Hakuna Matattoo though, if only he had taken me with him.

Thursday 19th January 2017

We did the sensible thing and took the 18th off, we needed a break from the booze and toasties diet, my insides were in pain. A top tip for anyone who ever visits Bangkok, Seven Elevens will save your life. Cheap water and exceptional toasties will get you through the worst of days. Find one and kiss the floor of it. We spent the night of the 18th in what was the hottest hostel room in the world a mile or so away from the strip. If it was any hotter, I would've been cremated. We all barely slept a wink and I will give you one guess as to who found this hostel. Tyrie was close to getting a hostel selection ban at this stage.

Being the unorganised shit-show of a travel trio that we were, we had no plans for the last four days in Thailand before heading over to Cambodia. In hindsight, we should've gone to Cambodia early, but instead, we decided to head to Pattaya, a coastal city south of Bangkok which looked lovely on the websites and leaflets. We did little to no research and jumped in a taxi to Pattaya, what sort of travellers gets a taxi somewhere? Idiot travellers that's who. We should've found a local bus and it would have cost us a tenth of the money. A long taxi journey in which Tyrie stopped at a public toilet and had to use his boxers as toilet roll and £20 each later we arrived in Pattaya, a place which I can now only describe as Thailand's unwiped ass.

We made a mistake here and we all knew it very quickly, but we could do absolutely nothing about it. This place was full of perverts, Eastern European man-giants and strippers with a massive street of bars thrown in for good measure. That afternoon we got our bearings, the strip of bars was lively so we were going to have a good look at it the next night, 'When in Pattaya' as the famous saying will never go. Somehow, I end up getting asked for a fight on the side of the beach just as the sun was setting. I don't know how to describe my fighting skills to you other than I have had two confrontations in my life and both times I have ended up on my backside. My signature move, if I were a wrestler, would be to curl up into a ball like a frightened hedgehog. This beast of a man who had just asked if I would like a fight was obviously incredibly hard and had quite a high chance of rearranging my face. I said no to him and to be fair he accepted that and walked up to the next bloke. I never saw him again, but I hope that he asked a very hard bloke for a fight and received a swift left-right-goodnight combination. Fight averted, beers and food had and Pattaya confirmed as an overflowing commode that we were going to go and drink lots of beer the following night.

Friday 20th January 2017

How to make the most out of a bad situation, by Harry Boucher, Ben Cheveralls and Callum Tyrie. That might be the title of my second book if this sales 10 copies. If there is one thing that university taught us it was how to make any night out decent. It is really simple actually, all you need is a pack of cards and too much beer. We purchased a pack of cards that had naked women on the front to keep the old perverts happy and proceeded to the first bar which was an Irish bar that we had scoped out. This bar was many things, but Irish was not one of them. 'Pint of Guinness please' I asked to which the barmaid responded 'Guinness' and looked at me blankly. Catfished and now sat in a below-average bar that didn't sell the drink that we wanted. Not the best start, but the beers were cold and the pool table was free so we got stuck in for an hour or so. As a little bonus ball, the middle-aged barmaid was exceptionally flirty. It was a shame that I could see the outline of her impressively large penis through her shorts. We didn't tip and got out of there pronto.

Next up on the Pattaya pub crawl was some live Muay Thai boxing. This was a street fight brought inside into a ring. It was surprisingly entertaining. I'm not a massive boxing/fighting fan, I don't mind watching the occasional 'Best Knockouts' compilation on YouTube I must admit, but I was expecting it to be a one beer stop for us. We ended up staying for four. Every single fight someone was getting knocked out with flip kicks and twist punches, it was incredible. These men and women went hell-for-leather from the first bell, like a drunken fight outside a kebaby back home, it was quite nostalgic. I was only some cheesy chips and beans away from being outside Star Kebabs in Yeovil.

We then entered the strip of bars named Walking Street which was wall to wall bars and strip clubs. By then we were half cut so it was quite appealing, lots of flashing lights, attractive women that were probably men and cheap beers. There was even a live music bar that had a reasonably average band playing some good songs. We should've stayed there all night. We had good seats and the beers were fizzy and not as flat as Adele's 2020 stomach like every other beer I'd drank so far in Thailand. But we had planned to bar crawl so that's what we did. We dived into every pub, bar and club that the street had to offer and ended up in some club that was rammed with people with swinging jaws and bottles of water. Knowing the trip I had on a malaria tablet I wasn't about to take a love heart-shaped pill off a random Swedish chap wearing sunglasses indoors. There were two bonus balls at the end of the night. Firstly, a genuinely great kebab on the way back to the room. Secondly, I didn't get found and beaten up by the nutter from the beach.

Saturday 21st January 2017

We went to an island off of Pattaya for a day trip, I needed to get out of the place. The boat to take us off the island was unnecessarily far away, it took us 25 minutes to walk there and I moaned the entire way. The island we visited was less of a shit hole than Pattaya itself but then a day trip to the sewer for a swim would've been a welcome break from there. The beach was nice and the water was clear but this wasn't going to change my perceptions of this little trip. As I soaked up the sun I was sick on the beach due to the hangover and malaria tablets not enjoying each other's company in my stomach. You shouldn't mix alcohol with these tablets, it was clearly stated and very well documented but I wasn't about to do this trip-of-a-lifetime sober or risk malaria. The occasional public puke was a side-effect I was willing to take.

Anyway, don't believe the flyers, Pattaya is a dumping ground for creepy golf holidays and slimy old men. The only reason you would like this place is if you are an actual pervert, in that case, you will be smiling and grunting the whole time you are there. Apologies if your grandad visits Pattaya for 'golf' or your husband does for 'work,' I can imagine this isn't the way you wanted to find out they're a disgusting pig.

Sunday 22nd January 2017

With little to no Google time, we found out there was a bus that would take us back to Bangkok for a total of £3.20. The same bus does the reverse trip, bearing in mind we shelled out £20 to get to Shitaya in a taxi. You can imagine the type of bus that sort of money gets you, it was an old shed on some wheels with flat tyres. The driver was either on the piss or genuinely wanted to kill everyone on board, he drove it as he stole it. A few very scary hours later and we were back in Bangkok. It turned out the driver was drunk, he had four empty cans of beer on his dashboard and was mumbling goodbye to everyone that got off the bus. The £20 taxi looked pretty good value now. Cambodia was fast approaching and we needed it, we had overstayed our welcome like a 5/10 one nightstand.

Monday 23rd January 2017

We hadn't seen the one thing that Bangkok is famous for, it's temples, so we decided to take a tour of as many as we could on our last day. The Grand Palace is the main attraction, so we went to see that first and I'll level with you, it was crap. I don't want to upset anyone who's gone to Asia and come back wearing elephant pants and meditating on a hand-woven mat. I just didn't get the temples, they did nothing for me. As an architectural design, it was excellent, as an experience, it was way below average. This also gives you an idea of what I thought of the other four temples we visited that day, they were not good enough. Once you've seen one temple you've seen them all in my book and this is my book. This day took an unexpected turn between temple four and five though which makes it worth documenting. Our guards were down and we got caught out big time! We were in a suit shop.

Mr Tim, our Tuk Tuk driver, had said to us earlier that day 'you want suit' to which we all replied, 'nope'. He had taken zero per cent of that on board and drove us to a suit shop which we got dragged into by some very eager men. There we were, sat in a suit shop with men measuring our legs and shoulders and everything in between. To keep these people from hating us immediately Tyrie and I engaged in conversation, Chevs was having none of it, he wasn't even making eye contact at this stage. There was a little seat in the corner that he sat in despite these men insisting he sat in one of the middle chairs with Tyrie and I. 'How much for a suit then?' Tyrie had asked the most open question you could ask in one of these shops. They said so many numbers within 30 seconds, the gist of it was about 3500 baht, £85 to us. An outstanding price for someone looking to buy a suit but far too expensive for three travellers. We shook our heads, told them no thanks and assumed that would be that, but they now wanted us to just buy a shirt. They were relentless and were starting to rub me up the wrong way by then, I wished I was sat in a corner chair out of the way.

The final straw was a man shouting in my face asking me how much I'd pay for the shirt he had in his hand. It was a nice, well-fitted shirt with thin blue vertical stripes, exactly the sort of shirt I wear to work nowadays. I'd pay £30 for it in TopMan no questions asked, but I wasn't in TopMan I was in Thailand. '100 baht!' I said straight-faced looking at this young man so he knew I wasn't joking. We were out of that shop within the next 20 seconds and everyone was furious with us and certainly swearing-in Thai as we left. I'd just offered the equivalent of £2.60 for a tailored shirt, I deserved to be called a few swear words but we needed to get out of that shop!

Mr Tim's attitude towards us changed after the suit shop incident. He was no longer our friend and didn't say a word to us on the way to the next average temple. He dropped us off, we walked around the temple, concluded it was rubbish and came out to find he had driven off and left us over three miles away from our hostel. Touché Mr Tim, Touché. He had made £20 out of us just for the Tuk Tuk driving but his head fell off when we didn't by one of his friends' suits.

The long walk home gave us all time to reflect. We concluded that Bangkok should have been a three-day visit entirely spent on Khao San Road avoiding ping pong shows. Silom and Pattaya are to be completely erased from my memory from now.

Cambodia

Wednesday 25th January 2017

We made it back from the temple that Mr Tim had stormed off from and left us at and the next day travelled East to Cambodia. I would describe our first border experience as pretty dodgy, there were a couple of bribes here and there, but we got through safely and made it to Siem Reap. There are some awful stories of travellers who have ended up having their passports taken from them and having to pay a lot of money to get them back from the border control. I'm not one for a confrontation so would have paid up without any argument had they taken my passport, they missed out on a few quid. The only reason Siem Reap is popular is because of Angkor Wat, a massive ruins of a temple that travellers and history lovers alike flock to see. As a so-called traveller, it was my duty to go and see the largest religious monument in the world whether I liked it or not. Tyrie had booked us into a below-average room yet again, however this time it did have a bar just across the road which we walked across too immediately for some flat beer. To the surprise of absolutely nobody, we ended up pretty drunk on our first night in a new place. We had decided that the best way to explore a place was to bar crawl around it, so that's what we did. Siem Reap was cool, it wasn't too built up and westernised like Bangkok and had some decent nightlife wedged in the middle of it. In the excitement of being drunk and in a new country we all ate some scorpions that a woman was selling on the side of the road and they were not bad at all. Anyone who goes on I'm A Celebrity and reacts badly to eating a scorpion is a liar and a fraud. Coronavirus wasn't a thing back then so eating scorpions was just funny and not potentially deadly. We ended up in an Australian themed bar and plugged in*. It was a great first night and it was lovely to be anywhere but southern Thailand.

*Plugging in is the act of sitting at a bar for a long period and charging yourself up with alcohol. It's one of my favourite hobbies.

Thursday 26th January 2017

The same Tuk Tuk driver who took us from the bus to our hotel the day before picked us up and dropped us to the boat for the floating village tour that Chevs had sniffed out. You can pay these drivers a weekly rate and they'll just chauffeur you about, it's brilliant as long as you don't get a driver like Mr Tim. We ended up with Chan Tao who's nickname was Santa. He was a good little driver and a reasonable tour guide too, he was only 17-years-old so I forgave him for not knowing the answers to all of my questions. The floating village was exactly what it says on the tin, a little village floating in the middle of a lake. There was a school, a local shop and everyone seemed to be pretty happy even though they lived on the water which is my worst nightmare. We donated some rice and it was quite a humbling experience without sounding too 'found myself', they didn't have much in this remote little village. The boy that was doing our tour was a bit of a geezer as well. If I had to guess his age I would've said he was 15 yet he was putting back beers like a seasoned regular at the local Wetherspoons. We bought a bag of beers from the floating shop and proceeded to get drunk on the boat back to the shore. At this stage, I was a functioning alcoholic covering it up with some fancy Instagram posts. We weren't as drunk as Santa though, he had settled into the drivers' bar where he had dropped us off and was sideways by the time we got back to dry land.

Now, I don't condemn drunk driving in any country, but we needed to get back to the hostel and there was only one way that was possible. God, please forgive me for my sins. Santa was worryingly good at driving a Tuk Tuk whilst intoxicated, this was almost certainly a regular thing for him. He informed us we had to pop to his village quickly to drop off some money which we said would be no problem at all. The village was 20 or so huts all-around a muddy field. The local kids were playing football, the adults were drinking and eating and everyone was having a great time, it was a real community and you could tell that they only really had each other and not a lot else. We were received like western kings, especially Chevs. Being six foot something and with long hair, he was like a mythical God to these people. Tyrie and I are only short, so we just fitted right in like it was our home. We played some football and Chan had some grub which was good because he needed to sober himself up before the final leg back to our hostel. Whilst he inhaled some rice and bread we were offered some wine which was not like any wine I have ever had before, rice wine they called it. I call it liver failure juice. If you'd like to taste something similar without having to travel to Cambodia and find Chan Tao's family, go down to your local petrol station, pull off the unleaded hose, ram it down your throat and pull the trigger. Rice wine did the job though and it was a good nightcap in the sense that it gave me no option but to go to sleep somewhere between the village and the hostel in the back of the Tuk Tuk and then for the next nine hours.

Friday 27th January 2017

I woke up feeling as fresh as could be, which was ideal because we were booked in for a beer pong tournament at the Aussie bar later that day. It was unlikely to be a sensible occasion and I was certainly going to get far too competitive over a game of throwing a ping pong ball into a cup. During the daily wander, we stumbled across a tank of small fish on the side of the street that would eat the dead skin off your feet, a strange cuisine for the fish. We all stuck our worn-out trotters in the water and let the fish eat the dead skin off. It was somewhere between torture and pleasure and not in a 50 shades of Grey kind of way. My feet certainly felt better as they slipped back into my now nearly sole-less New Balance trainers.

For unknown reasons we decided to pre-drink before the beer pong tournament and went to the bar over the road for a couple of liveners. The same woman who sounded like Kermit The Frog served us, she knew our drinks order and made a real effort to welcome us which was nice. We were locals and I quite liked it.

Later we arrived at the beer pong tournament which was a humongous sausage fest full of arrogant topless blokes who shouted as loud as they could and chest bumped each other far too much. In particular, there was a pair of lads from Denmark who were worryingly in love with themselves. They were the sort of blokes that wear a t-shirt a couple of sizes too small and take videos of themselves tensing and pouting. Tossers from right out of the top draw. Anyway, Tyrie and I played them in the quarter-finals and they stuffed us out of site. Writing this three years later I'm still incredibly annoyed about the manor we got dispatched and the way they celebrated the win. Their secret handshake and chanting following the victory made me debate completing a back one-and-a-half somersaults, tuck straight off the rooftop bar and onto the pavement below. Our pints were finished double sharpish and we stropped out of the bar. I wasn't going to sit and watch two pricks from Denmark win a beer pong tournament, I'd rather watch endless reruns of Cats, the new one!

They might have been better at beer pong, but I very much doubt they were better at getting twisted on cheap beers. The bars of Siem Reap spilt out into the roads and created a huge street party and we got right in the mixer. We got so drunk Tyrie had a panic attack and at one stage I was rehearsing how to tell his family that he had died on the side of the street after 15+ beers in Siem Reap. He didn't die, thank God because my speech to his family would have been terrible.

Sunday 29th January 2017

We went to see Angkor Wat and if I was to give it a TripAdvisor rating it would be two stars. It was scorching hot and granted, the hangover didn't help but it was just a load of old buildings. Don't get me wrong it is very impressive how they built it backalong* and it is pretty large, 402 acres to be precise, but that's all it is really, just big. Some people spend a whole week looking at this place, I was done with it after an hour of queuing to climb some stupidly steep steps that didn't pass my quick health and safety inspection. I think maybe if I went back now I'd appreciate it more, maybe I needed to do some sort of research to find out what was what. It means a lot to the Cambodian people as Angkor Wat is now on their national flag. 22-

year-old me was not arsed about it in the slightest, it kept me out of the pub though.

*Backalong is a time in the past. It can describe yesterday and it can also describe 1278

Tuesday 31st January 2017

If you are interested in getting a sneak peek into what Hell is like then fly over to Cambodia and take the hotel bus from Siem Reap to Sihanoukville, how they are legal is beyond me. This 'hotel' bus made every terrible hostel we had stayed in seem like a Hilton Hotel. As it pulled up I could hear a mumble of disappointment from everyone that was about to get on the bus and endure torture. We got on the bus at just gone. 9 pm, it was due at 8 pm so I was already annoyed. The driver was as miserable sod and informed everyone immediately that their belongings were not his responsibility and tough tits if they got stolen. Thank you very much for your excellent customer service! The beds were made to be shared despite them being barely bigger than a single and Chevs and Tyrie had drawn the long straws and were sharing which meant I was going to be lumbered with a random. I had everything crossed for a hot brunette. We'd talk for the whole trip, she'd have a soft spot for bald men, we'd fall in love, I'd sack my two mates off and travel with my new smoking hot girlfriend. Chance would be a fine thing. I got a lanky, smelly, British bloke who snored the entire way. At one stage I genuinely wanted the bus to crash to end the misery, it was either that or I was smothering lanky in his sleep with my pathetic pillow. I would rather spend eight hours speaking with Katie Hopkins than I would ever take this trip again, it was Cartel level torture. Here are some reviews that I read up after the trip about Virak Buntham, the bus company that I can only pray is no longer running. If I had read these before we would not have stepped foot on the bus. There are just the TWENTY SEVEN pages of complaints on TripAdvisor with an overall average rating of two stars. Two stars too many if you ask me.

"It is very difficult for me to stay polite describing this mess and it was difficult not to hurt any of these fuckers today."

"WARNING THIEFS ON BOARD!!! DO NOT USE VIRAK BUTHAM! The staff has stolen my phone while I slept!" I really hope they called the company BUTHAM on purpose, very immature and petty, I like it.

"I rarely write reviews and mostly good ones. But this company is from far the worst night buses company I've ever stayed in. No wifi, no toilet breaks. When changing bus, if you want to go to toilets you need to pay 1$ to stay in the worst WC ever, of course with no paper."

"Dangerous driving all the way of the journey, and he was on the phone most of the time. Please choose another company."

Oh Virak, just shut the company down you wanker!

Wednesday 1st February 2017

In the very early hours, we arrived in Sihanoukville and got to our hostel at 7 am. The good news was that the hostel looked wicked, we had done some research on this one. The bad news was we couldn't check in until 2 pm. I told the bloke behind reception how unbelievably tired I was and he replied, 'me too'. Fair one. I ended up catching an hours sleep in a tiny leather booth before people started waking up and coming in for breakfast. At the time this was the most tired I had ever been. I didn't sleep a wink on the night bus and had been on a two week all you can drink bender. My body clock and my body itself was in tatters. There was no way I could sit in the hostel bar all morning I genuinely think it would have killed me, so we stumbled down to the beach and slept there until the 2 pm check-in, checked in and then slept some more. My body was telling me not to leave the room again, I needed sleep badly. This wasn't a hostel known for its quiet nights in though, The Big Easy was a party hostel and you were either getting involved or getting pissed off. After a short debate between my head and heart I got involved, it was hard not too as they sold some huge beer towers for the equivalent of £10 which was good enough for us. Between towers, I met a chap who had broken his right arm and leg and was hobbling around on a single crutch. He had either had 15 beer towers to himself or had taken a little happy pill, he was completely off his rocker. If I was a betting man I would say that he had taken some ecstasy. It turned out he was there with his Mrs who was clearly in the pissed-off part of the hostel, he obviously had a death wish. He was less than bothered by this and I admired him for his humongous bollocks. He might still be in the doghouse now for it.

Thursday 2nd February 2017
   The only reason we went to the south of Cambodia was to visit an island called Koh Rong just off the coast of Sihanoukville. Koh Rong is a small island, just 78km2, with a big reputation for being lively. We had been warned that most people who visited came back with sickness and diarrhoea named Koh Rong Belly which was something to look forward to. By now I was pretty sure my insides could withstand anything as I had been drinking gone off flat beer for weeks, my organs were pickled. It was a little boat trip across to Koh Rong and on a half-decent boat, one that I felt was probably legal to make the trip unlike 100% of the other transport I had used so far. The first night we were set on having a couple of pints, some nice food and calling it a night and by some minor miracle we stuck to that plan. Chevs and Tyrie did a 'Joss Shot' which is by all accounts an illegal shot of alcohol. This consisted of pouring the Joss energy powder into their mouths followed by a shot of vodka, closing their mouths, shaking their heads to mix it all and then swallowing the lot. It is like having five Jäger Bombs and is theoretically a heart attack in a shot. I was thankful for being medically exempt from this shot because Chevs and Tyrie did not enjoy it at all. I messaged home to let them know I wasn't drunk and they thought it was a cover-up for being drunk. 'How long did it take to compose that text' my mum messaged back. My old dear has never had any faith in me staying

sober and with good reason. That night, we stayed in a beach hut which seemed like a good idea until it turned out to be an oven preheated to 220 degrees with no windows and no air conditioning. The waves outside were quite soothing though, in a way that I wanted to go and drown myself in the sea because I was so hot and couldn't sleep.

Friday 3rd February 2017

We had signed up for a spontaneous boat tour on our sensible mooch about Koh Rong the day before. It didn't take much to persuade us, some youngish chap spoke to us for a minute or so, said the words alcohol and barbecue and that was good enough for me to part with £30. We arrived and introduced ourselves to everyone on the boat, it was a mixed crowd of nationalities, ages and genders and then us three dingers*. It was an early start, 8 am meet at the boat, though it didn't feel early because I had been awake since 4 am in the beach oven.

The first boat trip took us across to an even smaller island than Koh Rong for a spot of lunch. To get from the boat to the island was like an Olympic High Jump event so we all had to help each other, and this was how we met the Pompy lot. I named them this because they were from Portsmouth, very imaginative. Alice, Tom and Laura made up this trio of mates, Tom and Alice were a couple and Laura was third-wheeling which I rated highly. I'll be honest, my first impressions of Tom was that he was going to be a nob. He was tall, ripped, tanned and had a wicked haircut which no one had in Asia because all of the barbers were terrible. 'He looks an arrogant twat' I thought to myself as I stared down at my belly. Within two minutes of talking to him, I took my initial judgement back. He was a lovely bloke. His better half, Alice, was a female version of him. They were like the Beckham's of Koh Rong only they were both very intelligent and had good degrees from proper universities. Laura had taken the piss out of us for struggling to get off of the boat and declared her love for a beer which meant we would all get along just fine. Anyone who can third wheel a couple on their travels is good enough to be a mate of mine. Chevs also fancied her which would make for some interesting drunk flirting from the big man at some stage. A pay-per-view event.

Back on the boat after some average vegetable rice, we set off to a beach that was said to be out of this world. It needed to be because the trip there was bloody choppy. Somehow, we got through the rough patch of sea and arrived at the beach. No beach is worth dying for but this one came pretty close, it was the first occasion that I was genuinely amazed by a location. The sand felt like velvet and the water was crystal clear. What a fantastic place to drink straight rum from a bottle with strangers and get wild. Things took a strange turn when one of the middle-aged women on the trip started crying. Thankfully there were a few good Samaritans on the trip including Alice and Laura who offered some drunk advice and she was soon back to being drunk and chirpy. I can't remember her name, but she was a lovely woman, I'm going to call her Amy. She had recently split from her husband and decided that she was going to take the positives and use her newly found spare time and money to travel. Hats off to her, she was as happy as I have ever seen any recently divorced human. I think my advice to anyone who has a little midlife crisis would be to travel, it's much better than a convertible. On the drunken boat trip back we stopped and did some snorkelling as some plankton lit up the sea and made it look like you were gazing up at the stars. I struggled to understand the point of this if I wanted to see something that was like looking at the stars I would just look up at the stars. I didn't want to go in the sea at all, it was a scary enough place in the day let alone in the dark of the night, but I eventually jumped in with a life jacket strapped on. It was good but I swallowed a load of seawater through the snorkel and my life flashed before my eyes.

Back in the safety of the boat, Amy suggested we went to her favourite restaurant for some food and most of the boat agreed other than a couple of miserable buggers that didn't like the idea of spending another second with anyone. These were the same people that didn't indulge in the rum on the beach. Rumour had it that the chef of this restaurant used to have a Michelin Star in Vietnam, but he moved to Koh Rong to be with his wife who used to serve his food, the things men do for high-quality skirt. His food was insanely good, I'd have been staring at a £100+ bill in England, just the £5 in Koh Rong. We proceeded to get even drunker with our new boat trip friends and I tried and failed to flirt with a French girl who was so far out of my league it hurt. A 'bonnet de douche' here and a 'bain-marie' there wasn't enough to impress her sadly. Chevs also tried and failed to flirt with Laura who dropped the 'boyfriend at home' bomb pretty early in his advances. All in all, it was a very successful night. I later found out that the chap running the boat trip was on the run from the English taxman. 'Good luck finding me here!' was his favourite saying. He made a good point, I doubt they'd find him doing boat tours on a tiny island off of Cambodia. Amy also slept with a man young enough to be her son that night, not any of us three, the midlife crisis was strong with that one.

*A dinger is someone stupid, another word for an idiot and a perfect adjective to describe me.

Saturday 4th February 2017

Koh Rong was an absolute pleasure. The boat ride back to the mainland was a bit bumpy and was not helping the hangover at all. Tyrie informed me that his insides were not ok, and I quote; 'Bouch I'm gonna shit myself if we go over another big wave.' I informed him he'd have to clench up because I couldn't control the waves as I'm not Poseidon. Thankfully his backside didn't explode all over the boat and we made it back to The Big Easy before he dropped the kids off at the pool. He dropped a lot of kids off at the pool actually, it was bedlam in the bathroom. Koh Rong belly meant that Tyrie was out of action so Chevs and I wished him well and proceeded to go and get beery. The Big Easy was the social hub of Sihanoukville which meant we could mumble our way through conversations with anyone and everyone over a tower of beer. We were informed of a beach party that was happening that night and needed no persuasion to attend.

The beach was lined with bars that spilt out onto the sand where most people were. It was very busy and I lost Chevs within an hour of getting there and we both proceeded to get drunk with a load of people we had met only a few hours before and made our way back in the early hours. Ben was about an hour after me and there was a very good reason for this!

Sunday 5th February 2017

Chevs didn't pull and he wasn't sneaking back into our room after giving someone 40 seconds of missionary. The reason he had stumbled in so late was much, much funnier. 'Why the fuck is my leg wrapped up?' Those were the first words to come out of his mouth that morning. I grumbled, got out of bed and walked across to investigate. 'You've had a tattoo mate.' I am no crime scene investigator but his right quadricep was wrapped tightly in cling film. I was certain that the hospital wouldn't have wrapped him like that if he had been stabbed or anything like that. It all flashed back to Chevs and the regret on his face was clear to see. 'Shit. Shit... Shit.' We unravelled him revealing what is to this day both the best and worst tattoo of all time.

I *heart* Bouch was in huge writing was tattooed across his right quadricep. I wish I took a photograph of his face as he looked down at the tattoo for the first time. I can't ever remember laughing so hard in my life, it hurt my jaw and sides so much. We had said we would get each other's names tattooed on us, but this was so much more than what was required. Even Tyrie who was somewhere between food poisoning and the morgue was crying with laughter. Why? What? When? Who by? Where? How? Are you mental? I had so many questions. This was a tattoo that Chevs was not so happy with. Even to this day he still informs me that he is going to get the I *heart* bit removed but this is yet to happen. Long live the tattoo.

Eventually, we all stopped laughing and packed our bags, we were travelling up to Kampot for the day and meeting the Pompy lot before heading to Phnom Penh. For some reason, we let Chevs book the accommodation in Kampot despite his head being removed from his shoulders. This was a decision we would regret four hours later when we arrived. 'There is only one person booked in' said the American owner of this snazzy little hostel. Tyrie looked at Chevs, I looked at Chevs, Chevs looked at his emails, Chevs said bollocks. He had kindly booked himself in for a night's stay and left me and Tyrie to sleep on the streets. Thankfully the owner managed to squeeze us into a double room which cost us a bit extra and meant I would be sharing with Tyrie, but it was a bed. Tyrie was still shitting through the eye of a needle so declined the offer to come on a moped ride with Chevs and me which was probably a sensible decision. Our hostel rented out mopeds, so we went and purchased two for the next 24 hours and shot off into the hills of Kampot. We had discussed potentially buying some motorbikes in Vietnam so being able to ride a moped was very important, we had both never ridden anything other than a bicycle before.

Twist-and-Go mopeds are just fast push bikes and involved zero pedalling, they are brilliant! We both enjoyed our first ever ride so much that we decided whilst overlooking Kampot at the top of a hill that we would be doing Vietnam on a motorbike. Whether they would be actual motorbikes or mopeds was yet to be decided, ideally a motorbike purely because I wanted to look cool. We rode the mopeds back to the hostel, got changed and went out for dinner with Laura, Alice and Tom. Tyrie said 'not a chance' to a ride on the back of my moped which was understandable considering I only had two hours experience riding one under my belt. Dinner was quick, we had no time for chit-chat, starters and dessert, United were playing and Tom had located a bar playing the game which was perfect. It was a good bar until they had an electrical fire in the first 20 minutes of the game. Despite the owner telling us this was ok we decided not to risk being involved in a massive explosion and advised him that he should probably call the fire brigade or at least an electrician. It was only us that left the bar so the locals were used to this sort of thing happening, a health a safety human would cry in that bar. The only other place playing the game was a restaurant that was as dead as Rolf Harris and about as popular. United won and we proceeded to play cards and have the chit-chat that was missed at the earlier meal. Kampot was a needed chilled stop, would I return? Absolutely not.

Monday 6th February 2017

I woke up and completed my daily checks; phone, wallet, necklace... ahh, no necklace, not ideal! I had left my necklace in the restaurant we had watched the game last night. This is quite important as inside the pendant there is all of my medical information should I have a heart attack. Luckily, I wasn't blind drunk the night before so I could just pop down and ask the barman to hand it back as I remembered taking it off and leaving it on the table we were sitting at. I still had my moped for the morning as well so getting the necklace back was going to be as easy as one two three, all I had to do was ride down, collect my necklace, ride back and Fox-Trott Oscar. It wasn't easy, it was like trying to seduce a nun. I arrived and asked the same barman that I had seen just 12 hours before if he had picked it up. He informed me that he had taken my necklace home with him last night for safekeeping, so he had stolen it. The necklace is worth nothing to anyone else unless someone in Kampot has also had a Ross Procedure but I highly doubted that. I started relatively reasonably asking him if he could pop home and retrieve the necklace and I'd pay the petrol but two minutes of him refusing to do this made me play the heart condition card. He eventually agreed to go and get my necklace. The only issue was that he lived an hour out of town, that's a two-hour round trip and our bus for Phnom Penh left in 45 minutes. Shit the fridge.

I needed this necklace so I paid the man more than he would get for the pawned necklace to go and retrieve it and asked Laura really nicely if she could collect it later that day as they were leaving on a later bus. We would be meeting again in Vietnam so I only needed to not have a heart attack over the following couple of weeks and I would be fine, easy. The likelihood of me having a heart attack is extremely slim as long as I don't bosh pints of red bull or sprinkle cocaine on my cornflakes. Laura agreed and all I could do was trust that the barman stuck to his word as I had just paid a premium for him to pop home and get it, £10 to be exact. He stropped off like the miserable bastard that he was and I rode back to the hostel.

Another very plush mini-bus trip later we arrived in Phnom Penh and checked into the hostel that was another very good find, we were getting quite good at booking rooms by then! On arrival Tyrie had his serious face on, he had something to tell us.

Tyrie

Tyrie was leaving us and heading back home to Essex. My initial response was 'Don't be a twat, Cal!' Tyrie has been a best mate of mine for a long time and a best mate of Chevs for even longer so we couldn't quite understand his decision. Did Chevs and I drink him into submission?

We had met initially back in 2012 in the lift going up to my university halls, he had an awful cardigan on and was carrying a crate of Budweiser. He asked if I would be interested in joining him in his mate's flat for a couple of beers, his mate was Chevs. I hadn't made a new friend at university yet, it was only a day in, I wasn't a loner weirdo I promise. I agreed to go to his mates flat but declined the beer. I have never lived down that initial moment when I declined a beer from Tyrie and Chevs, it is embedded in their memories. Once I got to know Tyrie better I told him that his cardigan made me want to puke and he needed to stop wearing it if he wanted to appeal to the opposite sex ever again.

Three years of university later and I had a best mate in Tyrie, in January 2014 we did four, four-day benders over four long weekends destroying us and our bank balances. I had watched him have panic attacks, score screamers playing football and pull a woman whilst wearing a West Ham shirt with Jarvis on the back. He is one of the only people I have met who I think is nearly as funny as me, his witty remarks and spot-on impressions make me laugh so hard no noise comes out.

You will notice that he wasn't hugely involved in the previous paragraphs and this was not common for him. He is usually the life of the party, the loudest and silliest person you could ever wish to meet. During the first few weeks of travelling, he had been a shadow of himself. He was homesick, and he had a girlfriend at home whom he missed. The only rule we had was to not get a girlfriend before travelling, not a difficult task for us idiots, but Cal had managed to do just that. I wish he pulled his head out of his ass and continued travelling with us, but his mind was made up. He was King Curtising us and would be packing his bags and leaving when we went to Vietnam. If you don't know King Curtis please take a break from reading and YouTube him immediately.

Tuesday 7th February 2017

The day that big Benjamin Cheveralls was pushed into the world by his dear Mother weighing 27 pounds or thereabouts. We had planned many beers later that day to celebrate however, we first wanted to go and visit the killing fields and S21. For those who don't know about the killing fields and S21, I will try and explain it as best I can but please bear in mind, I am not a historian, I dropped history in year 10.

It was an unbearably dark time in Cambodian history where the Khmer Rouge took over and killed over 25% of the population (2 million +) under the dictatorship of Pol Pot who is as horrid a man as there ever has been! The Khmer Rouge ruled Cambodia between the years of 1975 and 1979 and killed anyone who opposed them including children and babies. The killing fields that we visited first included an audio tour spoken by someone who had been there. The clue is in the name, this field was used to keep prisoners until they were brutally murdered by monsters with machine guns. They would play music loudly through large speakers so that the local people couldn't hear the mass murder happening only a mile or so away. The dead bodies would then be disposed of in a mass grave until the next set of prisoners were lined up and this would happen again and again and again. Unimaginable.

S21 is a prison that was previously a secondary school until the Khmer Rouge took over. The bastards that were in charge kept over 20,000 people behind bars over the years, starving all of them, torturing and killing many. It had been left relatively preserved which meant that I saw bloodstains on the walls and floors where prisoners had died. There were also some harrowing images of prisoners that had been killed by the guards, some by beating, some by gunshot, some by torture. I have never experienced anything like it, it was an extremely difficult morning but also very important to understand the recent history of this country and its people. I cried multiple times, it is genuinely heartbreaking stuff.

A grown-up discussion in the Tuk Tuk later, we arrived back at the hostel from our day out at around 3 pm and that made it beer o'clock on a birthday. We perched in the hostel bar and reminisced on the last few weeks with Tyrie who we would be leaving the next day. I was struggling to look him in the eyes, the Judas. As we were playing beer pong and laughing about some of the hell holes we had stayed in, a Bristolian chap wandered across and started talking to us. His name was Fred and he was just coming to the end of his travels like Tyrie only he had lasted longer than two weeks. Ok, that's the end of my bitterness. He informed us he had already overstayed by two weeks and needed to get himself home before his parents disowned him and his employer sacked him. Fred joined for a few beers and we instantly got on with him, he was very jealous that we were going to Vietnam and he was going to Bristol. Fred's couple of beers turned into many which resulted in him joining the birthday celebrations.

For Chevs 23rd birthday we went on a Strip Club Tour of Phnom Penh. There were two reasons for this. Firstly, they were everywhere and they served cheap beers and had free pool tables. Reason two is slightly more obvious, boobs. Just to clarify, strip clubs there are a lot different than those found in Europe, they are sports bars with half-naked women serving the beers and walking about the place. They would also take you to a private room for £10 and do much more than just dance for you apparently, I wouldn't know. We proceeded to have a pool tournament, playing a game of pool in every strip club we entered. Things got extremely lively and Chevs was suitably wobbling about and mumbling come the end of the night.

Thank god he wasn't on my team for pool because he couldn't see the balls let alone pot them.

Many beers in I mentioned to Fred that he should come to Vietnam with us. After some light persuasion, he agreed to come across to Vietnam. I just needed to persuade sober him that it was a good idea.

Vietnam

Wednesday 8th February 2017

My mouth was dry, my head was pounding and my stomach was full of cheap beer and dodgy street pizza. I couldn't see past this hangover, it is no exaggeration when I say I thought I was going to pass away that morning. The tiny silver lining was the fact that Chevs was in an equally awful condition. Sadly, I had no choice but to get over it as we were off to Vietnam that morning. My feelings were very mixed, I was miserable because of the hangover, excited as I was off to Vietnam and somewhere between sad and annoyed because I had to bid farewell to Tyrie.

Vietnam was a longish bus journey away and there was another border crossing that we had to navigate. This one was quick and easy and had a lack of bribing, how boring. We just gave our passports to the bus driver and he walked us through the border where a guard barely glanced at me and nodded to let me through. In my passport photo, I am a 16-year-old, baby-faced child with a full head of hair. The border control guy looked at it and then looked at me, a bald man with a large scruffy beard and didn't even give me a second look. There are a few horror stories of bus drivers holding peoples passports as ransom which would suck massively, but our bus driver was a decent bloke. His choice of in-bus entertainment was questionable though, some form of a Sci-Fi thriller with some giant spiders coming out of the snowy mountains. Credit where credit is due, he knew his audience and the locals loved it. The only issue with this trip was that the drop off point was two miles away from our hostel. This meant that we would have to get a taxi and they are very different in Vietnam. No cars, no Tuk Tuks, just men with their old, MoT-less, uninsured motorbikes telling you to jump on the back. It was a real take a deep breath and pray to every single God moment.

I jumped on the back of a motorbike with my rucksack on and Chevs did the same. I squeezed my rider like he was a nearly empty bottle of ketchup that I needed to get a final squirt out of. Two minutes later we were in peak Ho Chi Minh traffic and it was like nothing I have ever seen in my life. Thousands, potentially millions of people on their motorbikes swerving, beeping and shouting. Within the first few minutes, my rider had gone into the back of someone, proceeded to blame the other chap, stuck his middle finger up to him and just drove on. To be fair there was no one to blame, everyone was everywhere, it was every man, woman and child for themselves. There was a family of four on one bike, all just holding on casually like it was normal. Kids were on the back of bikes reading books and not even holding on. In Vietnam, this was the norm. Imagine trying to get a drink in a rammed bar but put everyone in that bar on a motorbike and make them all mentally unstable. That was Ho Chi Minh traffic.

It suddenly hit me whilst getting sideswiped by another bike that I was thinking about riding through this country. This wasn't getting chucked in the deep end, this was getting chucked in the centre of the ocean during a tsunami after having all of my limbs cut off. I'm not one to doubt my decisions but at that stage, I was doubting myself hard! Why on earth was I thinking of riding a motorbike through an entire country full of maniacs on two wheels? Rhetorical question, it's because I'm an twat.

We made it to our hostel in one piece. We needed to get our bearings and do some planning for this trip so Chevs and I settled in a local bar and discussed the places we wanted to visit and how long for. Our visa was for 30 days so we had a relatively strict schedule to abide by. Fred had messaged and was getting on the bus the next night and coming for two weeks of the trip confirming his sober head was just as carefree as his drunk one. We also knew that we would be meeting the Pompy lot somewhere in the North so we had to get up there in decent time. So, we decided that we would blitz the South and spend the majority of our time in the Midlands and the North of Vietnam ending up in Hanoi. It was either going to be Hanoi or a hospital along the way we'd end up in.

Thursday 9th February 2017

Travellers selling motorbikes in Vietnam is as common as a zoom quiz during the COVID-19 lockdown. Most people sell them either in Ho Chi Minh or Hanoi as this is the end of their journey and the start of someone else's. A quick search online pulled up thousands of adverts and every single one of them was shit heaps. We picked a few that were in the local area and went out to see what was on offer for a pair of novices about to be joined by another. On our way to view a pair of twist-and-go's we stumbled across three French guys sitting outside of their hostel with a piece of cardboard saying, 'Bikes For Sale.' We stopped and enquired and found that not only were these guys selling bikes, they were also extremely drunk. They were all motorbike riders back home and they assured us it was easy enough to learn. 'It's just like riding a bike', mumbled French Jake. He went to the garage below their hostel, started the bike up and rode it up the ramp to greet us. It was beautiful. An all-black Honda Win with a red star on the fuel tank, it was love at first sight. Charles went down to get his bike which was the same, just green and very, very loud. It had a custom exhaust on it which made it sound like the local antisocial boy racer. Jake and Charles gave us a quick drunk lesson on how to ride a bike. 'Left toe down for gear 1, up for 2, up for 3, up for 4. Left-hand clutch, right-hand break. Right foot big break. Twist your right hand and she will go. Good luck.' Good luck indeed Charles, we put their helmets on, hopped on board, started the bikes up and we were off. Time to learn how to ride a two-wheeled death machine.

Other than the fact I stalled immediately, I picked up the whole bike riding thing relatively quickly. It was a bit jumpy and not the quickest, but I was riding a motorbike in Ho Chi Minh. I lost Chevs immediately and proceeded to bike around the area mostly in second gear going 20mph or less getting regularly overtaken by mobility scooters. It was a lot of fun! I had an app called MapsMe (download it should you ever go travelling, no data required maps and directions #AD) which guided me back to the hostel of the French chaps. Chevs wasn't far behind and we were both alive so there was no discussion needed between us, we were both beaming from ear-to-ear after just 20 minutes on these bikes. We told the drunk Frenchmen that we'd take them.

Five minutes later I had transferred Jake 250 American Dollars (£200) and was the proud owner of a black Honda Win. Chevs did the same to Charles and our Vietnam journey had begun! We rode the bikes back to the new hostel that we were staying in that night and I felt like David Beckham pulling up on a Harley Davidson, other than the fact I was short, fat and bald we were the same person at that moment. I debated buying a leather jacket immediately as these bikes were the bollocks but Chevs told me he wouldn't ride with me if I did. Our new hostel was a good one as well, right in the middle of all the main strip of bars. You know Chevs and me well enough by now, we had just bought motorbikes and were in a new place, there was only one thing we were going to do that evening and it starts with G and ends with etting shit faced. We met a British lad in our room who was also keen for a few beers, it kills me that I can't remember his name because he deserves better than that. Anyway, Chevs, Raymond and I went out and got our drink on. Ho Chi Minh was an ok night out. There were plenty of bars, but they all seemed to be trying too hard and playing unbearably loud music with no lyrics, just constant thuds. The excitement carried us through and we arrived back at the hostel at 5 am and they had just started serving breakfast. We needed to get some beauty sleep because Fred was arriving in a couple of hours and we would be riding to a different place once he had purchased the third and final bike from the Tour de France squad, we were on a tight schedule. Bacon roll inhaled, I hit the hay excited to get back on the bike tomorrow for our first proper ride!

To put it into context, we had planned to ride a total of 1386 miles, almost certainly more once we took a few detours here and there. That's the equivalent of riding to Manchester from London seven times whilst on bikes capable of about 40mph on roads that weren't even close to being fit for purpose. As Chris Martin once sang, nobody said it was easy.

Friday 10th February 2017

Confirmation that Fred is a man right out of the top draw. He arrived at 10 am that morning, woke us up and we took him straight to the French who were extremely sad and hungover. Fred handed over 250 American Dollars, hopped on his new bike and was ready to ride. 'Learn on the way won't I.' He said to me as he put the key in the ignition for the first time. 'Well, you're in trouble if you don't Frederick.' I replied. With my bags strapped on, helmet on extremely tightly and feeling sick with nerves, a hangover and malaria pills, I was about to set off on an adventure to Phan Thiet, a coastal town where we would be staying in a beachside hostel. This would take three and a half hours in a car so we gave ourselves four and a half hours to get down there, five hours on a bad day. We left at midday so with all being well we would arrive at five o'clock which was the perfect time to grab some food. That's the ideal world that I was living in briefly, I was quickly reminded that travelling is not the ideal world especially whilst riding a motorbike poorly through an extremely busy city.

20 minutes into ride number one and I'd lost Chevs and Fred. I had a slight panic and was just pulled over on the side of the road praying that they rode past. Trying to spot them amongst the thousands of passing motorcyclists was the hardest game of Where's Wally ever. They didn't ride past or at least I didn't spot them. What a ball ache. My plan for the entire ride revolved around following Chevs because he had his maps on, this was supposed to be an easy ride. Instead, I had my phone out and was typing in Phan Thiet knowing that I was going to need to concentrate for the next however many hours. Panic half averted, I tapped in the route and it seemed simple, a highway would take me the whole way down. I just had to come off at the right junction. Pottering along I indicated and pulled onto a slip road which would lead me to the relatively straight highway most of the way to the destination. This riding malarkey was a piece of cake.

BEEP, BEEP, BEEP!! A Vietnamese chap was hanging out of his window, pointing at me and shouting, 'NO BIKES!' Are you having me on? A few moments later I reached a sign which was a motorbike with a huge red cross through it. I don't speak Vietnamese but I worked out for myself that the sign meant no bikes. I was up shit creek with the wrong directions. I turned around and rode back on myself, Vietnamese people were shaking their heads in disgust as they drove past me. I pulled over on the side of the road for the second time, I clicked the bike icon on MapsMe to see if it would change my route. It did, of course it did, what an idiot. The new route was slightly longer but if I got my head down I would still arrive by five-ish, emphasis on the ish.

Only 10 minutes into the new route and I found myself on the back of a boat wondering how it was all going so badly wrong. I was almost certain this was the wrong way, but I had no choice but to follow the directions. I asked a few fellow riders who I was squeezed up against on the boat, but they were all Vietnamese and did not engage in conversation with me. At this stage, I was a bit worried, for all I knew this boat could've just taken me straight back into Cambodia.

Across the river, I was still in Vietnam so continued to follow the map until it brought me to some large gates where guards were standing outside with big guns. I assumed they weren't just going to open the gates for me, but I double-checked. They put their hands up as if to say 'piss off' and I did just that very quickly as I wasn't in the mood to get shot between the eyes just yet. It was time for route three to get tapped in, the third time had no choice but to be lucky. I noticed that my phone battery was low. Luckily my bike, I had named him Reginald, had some USB points which I could charge my phone with, a very handy addition. Problem avoided, I pulled over to get my cable out which would keep my phone and my directions going and save me from getting even more lost and potentially dying.

There was a slight issue though, I had no cable, I could see it in the 'you stupid idiot' part of my memory still plugged into the wall at the hostel in Ho Chi Minh. This was a big problem and I entered full-blown panic mode very quickly, I was miles away from my destination in rural Vietnam and would have no directions in twenty minutes or so. There is only one thing to do in this situation and that is have a shout behind the helmet. I wasn't over exaggerating at this time and just accepted that I was going to die on the side of a road in Vietnam. To rub salt into my huge wounds I didn't strap my smaller backpack on to the back of my bike tightly enough after searching for the charging cable which led to it falling off as I rode off, this completely ruined my laptop that was inside. I was close to riding back to the guards and asking for that bullet between the eyes.

The only real hope I had was reaching some form of civilisation and hoping that someone had an iPhone charger that I could either borrow or buy. I pulled up at a petrol station in the hope they might sell one which they didn't, just petrol and some very dodgy looking meat available. I filled up whilst I was there just to be on the safe side as my bikes fuel gauge didn't work so it was complete guesswork as to how much fuel I had left. If I ran out of petrol then I was finished. I pulled myself together and rode straight for as long as I could. I had no concept of time or direction but I'm guessing it was just over an hour that I was riding for, it was enough to make my backside sore. I then pulled over to draw some cash out on the side of the road as another option I had was staying in a terrible roadside B&B for the night as it was getting darker by the minute. In the queue to get money out, I was saying 'Phan Thiet" to everyone, they all looked blankly back at me. I didn't even know if I was pronouncing it right, but I was trying every option. 'Van-V-Et?' 'Pan Th-it?' I was getting nowhere. Why didn't they teach me Vietnamese at school, stupid public education system! Then a little ray of sunshine joined me at the back of the queue in the form of an old lady smoking a cigarette and beaming from ear-to-ear. She said 'Phan-Thiet' but I was so tired and emotionally drained I thought she said 'Cigarette.' I don't smoke but I was going to die anyway so I said yes to the cigarette. She went into her purse, pulled out her phone and zoomed in on the map and said 'here?' I hugged her and she laughed at me, I was so excited I could've kissed her on her slightly hairy face. Maybe I wasn't going to die after all. She told me I needed to continue for another 45 minutes or so and I would reach Dat Do, she advised me to stop there and stay the night. I could have done with that cigarette she offered me, I had been on an emotional rollercoaster. Dat Do was a small town with shops and I would be able to get a new iPhone charger meaning I would be able to contact Chevs and Fred, advise them I was alive and well and then meet them the next day. Panic over, I flew the next few miles to Dat Do, it wasn't just my phone that needed recharging, so did my mental health.

Random cashpoint lady hadn't lied to me, I arrived and there were plenty of shops and bars for me to buy a charger and get some food. I went into the first techy looking shop I found, showed him my phone and he pulled a charger out for me. I asked if I could charge it quickly in his shop so I could phone my friends to which he kindly agreed. I went outside, sat on the steps and reflected on the last five or so hours of being lost and genuinely pretty worried. I can laugh at it now, but it was not funny at the time. The only positive was that I was now a pretty solid rider, every cloud. With my phone charged, I gave Chevs a WhatsApp message. He could receive them because he had a special Vietnamese SIM card in his phone, they didn't do these for iPhones which was not handy. I expected a message back saying no worries see you tomorrow, but he messaged me back saying 'see you in 20 minutes, just behind you.' The state of it.

Half an hour later Chevs and Fred arrived at the shop I was still sat outside of. I was relieved to see them as a few hours ago I was irrationally thinking that I would never see them or anyone I loved again. I was also incredibly confused as to how they ended up taking longer than me to get to this place, I had cocked up beyond belief. It turned out that Fred's bike broke down almost immediately explaining how I lost them so early in the trip. It had been fixed on the side of the road by a very helpful Vietnamese chap, but then they also made the same mistakes as me and drove onto the highway where they were also told to turn around. This was the worst start to a road trip in history and we were still three hours away from our actual destination, Phan Thiet. It was gone 6 pm and darkening quickly, the clearest advice that we had received when talking to people and Googling the different routes was to *never* ride at night. Tired bus drivers had wiped out plenty of travellers and locals on their motorbikes over time and we did not want to become part of these statistics.

Stupidly, we ignored the advice and there we were, riding our bikes at night. I am not sure as to why we decided it would be a good idea to complete the journey, our pride was already damaged enough to call it a day halfway. I'm sure we aren't the only ones to have messed this journey up.

The two-hour trip from Dat Do to Phan Thiet took well over five hours, Fred's front light stopped working about halfway through so he had to ride between Chevs's at the front and me at the back. I had to go at the back because Chevs's brake light wasn't working. Just in case riding at night wasn't dangerous enough we were doing so with two lights between us. Fred's bike eventually completely stopped working five kilometres from the hostel that was going to be closed by the time we arrived. The final stretch was painfully slow with Fred pushing his bike up hills and coasting it for as far as he could down the other side. It was a nightmare of epic proportions. A four-hour trip had taken us 12 hours, we had got lost, broken down, been on a boat and risked our lives by riding at night through Vietnam. It was as dangerous as people said, buses were speeding on the wrong side of the road and lorry drivers liked to play a game called 'how close can I get to the motorbikes.' When I arrived at the hostel my bum was as sore as a man who had received a prostate examination from a giant. My spine was a stack of loose pebbles and my morale was at an all-time low. I was ready to set Reginald on fire and never get on a motorbike again. The only thing keeping me going was the thought of how comfy bed was going to be. The icing on top of the shit-filled cake to end the day was the hostel being shut and not being able to find anyone on the reception to let us in. Three blokes standing in the dark in Vietnam completely broken. At this stage, everything was garbage.

Saturday 11th February 2017

The receptionist was found at 3 am so we did manage to get some sleep. Bed, as imagined, felt like a memory foam cloud of happiness despite it being a wafer-thin mattress on the floor. As I led down and rested my head on the pillow, I let out a huge sigh that is usually reserved for an orgasm. Seconds later I was away with the fairies. When I woke up and opened the door of our hut, I was pleasantly surprised, the place was more of a beach resort than a hostel and we had a lovely view of the sea. It was nice to breathe some fresh air after inhaling my breath for 12 hours yesterday under the helmet. I was fully aware that Phan Thiet didn't have much to offer, Google had told me that, so it was important to ensure that the essentials were sorted. Fred got his bike into a mechanic and bought some weed from that very mechanic so we went down to the beach for the most well-earned relax I have ever had. I quite fancied a dip in the sea but on arrival, I observed that the waves were at least 3 feet high and crashing in so I decided to boycott that plan, I didn't fancy drowning. There were a few kite surfers about but other than that it was relatively quiet. Why anyone thinks that attaching a kite to their surfboard is a good idea is beyond me. It looked as fun as sucking up cow pat through a straw. Fred rolled a humongous joint and we indulged and chilled the eff out. I had only ever smoked weed once before at university but acted like I was Snoop Dog and puffed away saying that it was 'good stuff.' I had no idea if it was or not, I was barely inhaling anything. The relaxed vibe was spoiled by the planning of the next days ride to DaLat, a town right at the top of a mountain. The thought of having to jump back on my motorbike and ride up a mountain for somewhere between two and 14 hours was sickening. We had made our beds, time to lie in them.

Sunday 12th February 2017

As we left for DaLat all of our bikes were in working order which was a good start to the day. Fred's worryingly cheap mechanic had fixed his bike, how long for no one knew. I had a positive outlook about the ride and I was certain it was not going to be as bad as our first effort. I was correct, it wasn't as bad, but it was quite bad. Yet again we lost each other within the first 20 minutes of being on the bikes. This time it was completely down to our incompetence as the roads weren't even busy. I made my way to the bottom of the mountain and waited, assuming that they would pass me at some stage. That never happened. I had a quick chat with myself and decided that they had probably got onto the mountain before me via a sneaky shortcut or something, so they would've been way ahead of me. Yet again I was riding solo.

My ride was relatively uneventful, the views were incredible and DaLat was very well signposted so there were no stresses. There were a few stretches of steep mountain where I thought Reg wasn't going to make it to the top but he chugged away in first gear and got the job done. I found that not stressing about directions and potentially dying made riding considerably more enjoyable. I arrived in DaLat and got hold of Chevs and Fred when I connected to the WiFi of a local café. They were somehow behind me again and told me they would be at the hostel in half-an-hour so to meet them there. Maybe they just didn't like, it felt like they were avoiding riding with me. When they arrived at the hostel I noticed that both of them had cuts on their legs and arms which was a result of falling off their bikes. They informed me that they had been involved in a small pile up at the bottom of the mountain when another bike slammed on the breaks resulting in Chevs going in the back of them and Fred going into the back of them both. I checked they were both ok before laughing, they weren't laughing as much as their cuts and grazes were pretty sore. The accident hadn't caused any damage to the bikes mechanically, the tape was holding strong. This little mishap couldn't slow us down, so the brave soldiers showered, cleaned their wounds and we all headed out for an exploration of this quaint mountain town.

DaLat is the sort of place that quirky people would like, you know the ones who wear floral headbands and flared trousers. Your parents would like it too and probably your grandparents. It was a place full of character. Here's a Harry fact for you, Da Lat was developed as a resort by the French in the early 1900s which went a long way to explaining why it resembled a French town so much. Consider this book educational! One thing it did have was a buzzing night market with lots of food stands, wavey garms and music. We all instantly regretted only having one-day planned here, on reflection it should have been a two-day trip at least. The highlight of our whistle-stop-tour was Fred taking over the microphone of a street busker and giving everyone his rendition of Wild Thing. He was a crap guitarist and an average singer, but he was definitely a showman. 'Scream if you wanna go faster' he shouted at the crowd of about 30 people who were all loving it. 'Wild thing... You Make...' he struggled to find the next chord... 'My heart sing!'

Monday 13th February 2017

Can I shock you? For the first time, we managed to stay as a trio for an entire journey from DaLat to Nha Trang which was our next destination. It was a relatively uneventful ride other than Fred and Ben the motorbike men both falling off again. This time it was more of a skid to a stop which resulted in them rolling off their bikes, no damage was done although their egos had taken another hit. We were all a bit tentative after the crash, the mountain road was 95 per cent smooth, the other five per cent was randomly located massive potholes big enough to tip over a military tank. We rode past an ambulance that was attending to a motorbike accident and judging by the state of the motorbike I medically declared the rider dead at the scene. I wouldn't like to guess how many people die as a result of falling off their bikes in Vietnam, Google thinks only 14,000 a year but that figure seems a bit 'one-two skip a few, 99 14,000' I would be shocked if the real figure isn't triple that at least.

Safely at the bottom of the mountain, we entered Nha Trang and it was unexpectedly busy. We made it through the traffic without losing each other however, I had lost something much more important, my sunglasses. My Meller sunglasses or Naughty Mellers as I liked to call them had hardly left my face the entire time I had been travelling. They were tortoiseshell with some bright blue mirrored lenses and I loved them more than most family members. I had taken them off whilst at a set of traffic lights so I could get a better look at the map on my phone, but the wait was a lot shorter than expected. I got beeped at which made me panic and speed off watching my Mellers fall from the fuel tank and onto the road to get crushed by the following bikes. This was genuinely devastating and it is not an overreaction when I tell you that it was the worst thing to happen to me in my entire life. Now I was going to have to buy some fake Ray Berries from a street stall and look like every other basic traveller in Vietnam. Ugh.

Emotionally unstable, I checked into our hostel and found pure happiness written upon a cardboard sign. 'Free Pints from 5-7'. A happy two hours was commencing very shortly and that was a massive slice of me. We chucked our bags in the hostel room which was full of Australian's who were also heading downstairs for plenty of beers. They were typical Aussie's, drunk, laid back and up for a laugh. They informed us that there was a pub down the road that did cheap beers for afters. 'You can have a night out for five bucks here cunt!' They mumbled. For those who aren't aware, cunt is not a derogatory term in the Australian language, it is their way of saying, mate. Say no more, we became honouree Australians for the night and joined them in getting very loose. Free pints until the barrel ran out at the hostel and 25 pence for a pint at this other bar was biblical. That's the cheapest we'd found so far. Not bad Nha Trang, not bad at all.

Tuesday 14th February 2017

Nha Trang isn't a bad place but there isn't much going on. If it was an English football team it would be Everton, trying hard to become something but just not quite achieving it. We were staying for two nights simply because the hostel was good and the beer was sometimes free and if not it was cheap. One thing that was nearby was Vinpearl Island which was accessible by either the World's highest or World's longest cable car, I think. It might be as unimpressive as the longest cable-car in Nha Trang for all I know but what I am sure of is there was a reason why we went on it. The cable car took us across to Vietnam's budget Disneyland which was a half-decent water park and a few attractions. It wasn't worth the trip over but coming back across on the cable-car at night was quite nice.

That night I received a £1.40 haircut on the side of the road which was utterly crap considering all he had to do was shave the little hair I had completely off. He shaved me down to a grade one and then proceeded to cut-throat my already receding hairline even further back! We had some cheap beer but it was very low key compared to the night before. We got ourselves into bed just after midnight as we had a trip to Quy Nhon the day after and we needed to be on the road relatively early. My sleep was disturbed three or four times by bolloxed Australians stumbling back in from another mad one, I'll never be angry at drunk people returning to a hostel because I was one of them a lot of the time.

Wednesday 15th February 2017

Let's skip the early rise and average breakfast and get straight to me on the side of a road with a snapped chain on my motorbike shouting *fuck off* at it like a mad man. Thankfully we had all managed to stay in a group for the first couple of hours of the ride so the lads were able to stop and assess the damage with me. We weren't mechanics but the chain being in half and hanging down on the road suggested that it was broken and all three of us were in agreement. We still had about three hours of riding to complete that day so we needed to get this sorted sharpish. My bike was the only one not moving although Fred's had no front light and Chevs only had full beam so they would be useless should we have to ride at night again. Chevs suggested that he and Fred rode to find a mechanics so I watched the only two people I knew for about 1000 miles ride off into the distance. I began walking up the side of a relatively busy road muttering obscenities to myself. Five minutes into my push a man pulled over in front of me on his motorbike and came over to offer some help. He couldn't speak any English, but he grabbed hold of my chain and looked at me as if to say 'that's fucked.' Fully aware thanks mate, please help. 'Mechanic? Fix? Fix Chain?' I said to him hoping that he understood. Accompanying my attempt to have a conversation with this lovely man was a lot of rubbish hand jesters. It seemed to get through to him though as a few minutes later he was pushing me along the side of the road. He had his right foot off of his bike and on the back of mine pushing it along. The Vietnamese people are brilliant, everyone seemed willing to give a helping hand at any time of day and they would do so with a smile.

Ten minutes later I was in some blokes shed that had half-a-billion bike parts inside. Not only did he have a new chain for my bike he also had the best WiFi I've ever experienced, in the middle of nowhere, Vietnam, how?! I only get two bars from Sky in Yeovil now and have to watch episodes of Brooklyn 99 in four parts. This allowed me to get hold of Chevs who came back to meet me at the shed, Fred had ridden on as he didn't want to be riding at night with no light which was an incredibly sensible idea although somewhere in this guys shed was a working front light for Fred I was sure of that. It cost me all of £3.70 for the new chain and fitting.

The big man and I were back on the road and absolutely flying towards Quy Nhon, my chain had clearly not been working from the start as I could go about 20 miles an hour faster now on my new racing chain. I was only some go-faster stripes away from breaking the land speed record. It was only a matter of time before we caught up with Fred and could cruise into Quy Nhon like we were on Sons of Anarchy, I was Jax Teller.

Happiness cut short, we were back on the side of the road with Chevs's bike and this time it was very broken. No matter how many times we kicked it, prodded and turned the key it was not starting for love nor money. We walked for 15 minutes before a man shouted at us from his front garden speaking pretty good English and asked us if the bike was broken. My sarcastic and tired head wanted to reply, 'no mate we are just taking our bikes out for a little walk!' But realised this was not the time for sarcasm. *Help us!*

This was going to take a couple of hours, it was no quick fix. The man informed us it was probably best if we went to get some food and drink from the local shop whilst we waited. The local shops sandwich selection didn't take my fancy as they had bugs all over them, so I just got a bag of ready salted crisps and a Fanta, the lunch of kings. His family were extremely welcoming and offered us a seat whilst we discussed how incredible it is that everyone in Vietnam could just fix your bike. They all seemed to have a screwdriver in their back pocket and could just tighten a few screws and send you on your way. We also laughed at the fact we would yet again be riding at night again and that our luck was probably going to run out and we were likely to get mowed over by a lorry later on. Happy thoughts. Two hours passed and the bike was fixed and back to its unsociably loud self. Everything crossed for a safe and breakdown free road to Quy Nhon!

I don't know how many people were looking over us but we somehow made it to Quy Nhon alive. The roads were horrible single carriageways on which lorries would overtake busses on corners and therefore be driving directly at us. It didn't matter if they were on a straight or a completely blind corner, they'd overtake. It also didn't help that Chevs was beaming everyone the whole way. This pissed off the oncoming traffic and resulted in a lot of beeps and middle fingers directed at us. We coasted into Quy Nhon and headed straight to the hostel that Fred had found for us. He was sitting outside with the manager of the hostel having a pint and looking very relaxed and stress-free. I inhaled a pint quicker than I ever have before on arrival, I was so thirsty and so tired from another 10-hour journey. Fred cheered us up with the outstanding hostel room he had booked for us, we had a double bed each. Having a double bed to yourself as a budget traveller is euphoric, it was like going out expecting to pull Susan Boyle but ending up with Rita Ora. Before star-fishing the bed it was vital that we had some food and a liquid that wasn't beer alongside our beers so we popped to the local restaurant and did just that. The bed was yet again ridiculously comfortable once I eventually got into it, heaven in a hostel.

Thursday 16th February 2017

One thing that needed sorting that morning was the bikes, again, and properly this time not just with a screwdriver and some duct tape. We only had one fully working front light and a lot of clunks and whistles coming from different locations, the bikes weren't going to get us anywhere near North Vietnam at this rate. The hostel manager advised taking them to his mate who would do all the work required for a packet of crisps and a toastie, so we rode over to him. He informed us that these bikes needed a service and a few parts changing which would take a few hours. This wasn't ideal as we were supposed to be riding up to Hoi An that day. We agreed that it was best to stay in Quy Nhon for an extra night so popped on to our good friend Google to see if there was anything to do there. Google confirmed there was absolutely nothing to do there. We went for the next best thing and decided we would go and stay at the highest rated hostel in the area. It was called 'Life's A Beach Backpackers' and would only cost us £7 for a night which was good enough for us. We booked ourselves in and went to a little sports bar for some lunch whilst the bikes got some tender love and care as we had given them none. The mechanic worked his magic and the bikes were all closer to being road-legal although still certainly not.

We arrived £20 lighter riding the smoothest motorbikes in Vietnam to Life's A Beach Backpackers. Can I shock you? It was on a beach. I say beach, it was more of a cliff with some sea at the bottom, the beach was not accessible and you would not want to sunbathe on, you would get swept away to sea immediately and drown. We were greeted by an English chap who had built the hostel with his friend. They had travelled to Vietnam and fell in love with the country and decided to live and open a business here. A huge risk but he seemed pretty happy and content although, they were both very much separated from their wives and only saw their kids at Christmas. That is what it is. It wasn't luxury by any stretch of the imagination, but the place had a lot of character. The central part of the hostel was the open planned bar that overlooked the sea and offered a half-decent view. It was full of backpackers and up to that point, it was the best hostel I had stayed in. It helped that we expected absolutely nothing of it, a true underdog story, like Yeovil Town getting to the Championship. Even though we had to be up early and on the road we drank until the early hours. The bar shut at midnight but then the bar staff just joined in the drinking games until we all eventually dropped. There was a lot of free drinks being handed out which did make me wonder how profitable this place was.

Life's A Beach was a top establishment, it made the two days stopover worthwhile and the eggs and bacon in the morning were greasy and I loved it.

Friday 17th February 2017

I expected nothing of street food in South East Asia yet had been very impressed by the quality of it throughout Vietnam so far. We would pull our bikes up anywhere and they'd make a lovely chicken and rice or a decent noodle dish. Whether it was chicken was a whole different matter, but it was certainly nice although sometimes way too spicy! When we pulled our bikes over for some lunch that day we expected the same, an alright meal and if we got lucky it would be nice. We each bought some chicken and rice which is always a little bit risky but we had grown to trust the street chefs by then. All that trust was lost in this street-side café. As we sat in this roadside dungeon, a lovely old lady served us some roadkill chicken and a big bowl of undercooked rice. It still had its fucking beak on! The poor thing was probably still clucking around outside 10 minutes before we arrived.

We didn't eat a single bite as we didn't fancy a serious case of salmonella, paid up and headed to the next place that was serving food. We stumbled across a café that looked slightly more established and jumped in for a coffee and a panini which were both equally as nice. I had noticed across Vietnam that the coffee was fantastic, I'm not a massive coffee drinker but this stuff was good and very sweet! The coffee would slowly drip into the cup below and would be thicker than the coffee that I was used to back home.

Refuelled, we set off and got to Hoi An in decent time. It was an easy ride because Chevs was leading and doing all the directions. I say easy, it wasn't as I had managed to lose him two out of the three rides so far. The roads were also safe and relatively quiet which was a bonus. We arrived and parked up outside our hostel and checked ourselves in. Hoi An was a place that everyone spoke very highly of so we were keen to get out and see what it was all about. By that I mean we were ready to go and straight-arm-finish plenty of beers. It was a buzzing little place full of hostels, bars, cafés and pubs. We popped into a little pub on the side of the road for a burger and a pint deal that cost me a huge £1.50. The burger itself was nice but the pint was anything but. If you did the washing up with beer instead of water and then drank the beer from the sink afterwards that's what I was drinking. Over the river was where all the clubs and lively bars were so we made our way across once our food had gone down and we somehow sipped our way through the pints. This was the first time in Vietnam that I had encountered club reps trying to talk people into going into the bar that they worked at. If you hand out flyers for a nightclub anywhere in the world you are a loser. I know this because I did it during my time at university in Southampton and got called a 'fucking loser' quite often. A gobby wannabe geezer with a shit haircut talked us into going into a bar named 'Mr Beans Bar' which was, as the name suggests, quiet. It did serve incredibly cheap buckets though, so we sucked up a few of them and they got us where we needed to be pretty quick. We spent a good few hours in this bar playing pool and chatting to people, it did get busier thankfully. We met a lot of people that were travelling the opposite way so we could discuss with them what was worth doing further up the country. By the sounds of it, the North of Vietnam was the place to be! We informed them that the South had been pretty average actually which wasn't the news anyone wanted to hear.

I now know why the bar was called Mr Beans, it was because it left people unable to speak, very creative. On the stumble home, we found the famous Bahn Mi Queen who, if rumours are correct, serves the nicest Banh Mi baguettes in the whole country. A Bahn Mi is Vietnam's answer to SubWay only they don't call themselves sandwich artists. At that time I was so pissed and hungry I would've eaten the rice and beak from earlier on so this meat-filled baguette was to die for. I made a drunk mental note to ensure I tried one sober as well before we left.

Saturday 18th February 2017

Hungover and hungry we popped to the café across the road for some breakfast. Fred wanted to buy himself a suit and send it home for when he got back in a week or so in the hope that he still had a job to go to. If not, he was just going to be suited and booted sitting on his sofa. Chevs and I were still suffering from PTSD from the Thailand suit shop experience so would not be buying a suit but did agree to go with Fred and give our honest opinion despite being fashion disasters ourselves. The suit shops in Hoi An were considerably better than the backstreet shit-shop we went to in Bangkok. I don't think I'm exaggerating when I say there were thousands of materials to have a suit made out of in this shop. The woman explained to Fred that it was about £150 for the suit to be tailored and it would take two hours of his time now and then a day to make. That was our cue to leave Fred to it and go for a little explore.

I found myself agreeing with what everyone had said about Hoi An, it was a place full of characterful buildings and quaint little shops and cafés. A lot of these shops were full of clothes and they were of the waviest variety. They seemingly made the shirts by hanging them up against the wall and just lobbing a load of paint over them. We treated ourselves to some shirts and shorts and then jumped into a café for a coffee and world-class slice of banana bread. When we arrived back at the suit shop Fred was £150 lighter and the proud owner of a tailored suit.

Later that day we decided that we would visit the night market which was back across the river by Mr Beans. This was the perfect place to buy some gifts for the family and send them home in the hope they hadn't forgotten all about me. The market wasn't great, everyone was selling the same things just on different stalls, it was like a Scooby Doo sketch. Backpack, fridge magnet, shorts, backpack, fridge magnet, shorts. Although the market wasn't as good as expected I managed to pick my sisters up some handmade backpacks that were pretty cool and I bought mum and dad a painting that a blind lady had done in front of me on the street. The painting wasn't very good, just a lot of splodges. Amazingly none of these gifts made it home. One backpack I had to use when mine broke and it lasted about three days before breaking itself. The other backpack was left in a hostel in Laos and the painting was left at the bottom of my rucksack for weeks and when I pulled it out it looked like a two-year-olds effort at painting a dog. The thought was there though. I ended up getting them absolutely nothing, not even a postcard, what a shit bloke.

We drank much more sensibly that night and met a couple of people that Fred had met during his time in Laos, it is always nice to get peoples thoughts on places and their thoughts on Laos was that it was crap. This also gave us a chance to see all of the lanterns that light up the streets of Hoi An which is what it is famous for. Streetlights would be more beneficial, but the lanterns did look nice. Most importantly, it gave me a chance to have a sober Bahn Mi from the Queen and it was elite scran.

Sunday 19th February 2017

We were only heading to Danang that day which was 40 minutes away, even we couldn't mess that journey up! With that in mind, we went to pick Freds suit up and booked ourselves on a boat tour of Hoi An before leaving. Back in the suit shop Fred went behind the curtains and came out in a grey, fitted suit which was like something Conor McGregor would wear. It was weird to see Fred looking smart as I only knew him as a scruffy traveller, I forgot that back home he was a normal human with a normal job and life. I told him that he looked a million Vietnamese Dong (£34.30) and he purchased the suit and had it sent home. We walked across to our boat tour and on the way I spotted an old lady selling bananas and offered to give her a hand with carrying them. She was only about five-feet tall and the weight she was carrying was substantial enough to make me huff and puff so around 100kgs. I managed to sell zero bananas for her but did buy six myself despite not wanting them at all. She scammed me.

The boat tour was an unfitting end to our time in this ace little town. It was about as informative to me as BBC Bitesize Science would be to Professor Brian Cox. This didn't change my view on Hoi An though, it was definitely worth the visit and I will be visiting again in the future that is for sure and will be buying a suit!

We did manage to ride to Danang with no hiccups that night but there wasn't anything to report there other than a bridge shaped like a dragon.

Monday 20th February 2017

The reason we had stopped in Danang was that we were riding the Hai Van pass to Hue and wanted to be well-rested before leaving. It is said to be one of the best roads in the entire world and if you are a Top Gear fan (the good one with Clarkson, Hammond and May) you would have seen them ride this road on old scooters. Top Gear riding the Hai Van pass has only made it more popular and it was something that I was properly excited to do now I was a hardcore biker. If you are a fun sponge* you can just jump on the back of a tour guide's motorbike and do the Hai Van pass, there is less chance of falling to your death that way.

Bikes full to the brim with petrol we set off on this twisting and turning mountain pass and it did not disappoint. The views were unbelievable and the roads were mostly smooth which is very rare in Vietnam. There were also no lorries and buses allowed on this pass which meant we were safe from death by being run over. My only regret was that poor old Reginald wasn't the fastest of bikes, I would love to go back and ride a more powerful bike through the mountains. Words won't do this ride justice so I am just going to say that it was the best couple of hours I spent on my motorbike and if I ever ride/drive on a better road I will be astonished.

On the other side of the pass we rode into Hue, another small town that didn't on paper have too much to offer. There were a few things that needed to happen in Hue, some happy, some annoying and some sad. The happy was it was my 23rd Birthday on the 22nd of February so Hue would involve a monumental piss up of the highest order. The annoying was that I had a hole in my exhaust meaning that it was now louder than Chevs's air raid siren of a motorbike, that needed fixing. Sadly, Fred would be leaving us on the 21st, his time as a traveller had now officially come to an end and he had to get back to Brizzle for work. All good things come to an end. As it was Fred's last night, we were going to drink ourselves into oblivion and make his flight home very uncomfortable due to a large hangover.

Our time in Hue started poorly as Chevs had booked us into a hostel that no longer existed and hadn't done for quite some time. We arrived at the said hostel which was now a massage parlour which looked like it offered happy endings as well. In hindsight maybe we should've stayed there. The not hostel, hostel turned out to be a blessing in disguise because the only other hostel with rooms available was Vietnam Backpackers and this place was GOAT!^ On arrival, we found out that it was ladies night at the hostel bar which involved dress up and drinking, we didn't need an excuse that night but it helped us along the way. The bar crawl from the hostel took us to the two other bars of Hue, DMZ bar and Brown Eyes. What sounds like the worlds shortest and shittest bar-crawl turned out to be insanely good! Hue was like a small university town during fresher's week. Everyone there was in the mood to get drunk and the bars knew exactly how to ensure that everyone was, mainly by pouring straight spirits into people's mouths. Fred pulled that night and woke up next to a lovely female. I woke up with a pint by the side of my bed with a headache that hurt my eyes. Chevs hadn't made it to bed he was just led on the floor next to his bunk which was a mental decision from him. The battle scars in the form of two stamps from DMZ and Brown Eyes were clear for all to see. Brown Eyes was the first decent club I had been in whilst away, it played great music, had good drink deals, was rammed and had an excellent smoking area, the key to any good pub/bar/club. We'd be back no doubt.

*A fun sponge is someone that isn't interested in having fun and manages to suck the fun out of everyone else, not sexually.
^GOAT means the greatest of all time. It is most commonly used to describe Cristiano Ronaldo and Lionel Messi. I describe things such as LIDL lasagne and Scott McTominay as GOAT.

Tuesday 21st February 2017
The only reason I got out of bed that day was to say goodbye to Fred. He was extremely hungover and stunk of booze so I was satisfied that his trip home was going to be terrible. He had sold his bike to a poor lad going the other way who was going to have all kinds of problems, that bike was awful and was held together with chewing gum and Sellotape! With a hug and good luck, Fred was off in the back of a Taxi to Hue Airport. Fred was a rare bird and people like him don't come along very often. Can you imagine meeting two lads in Cambodia that you have never met before and agreeing to ride half a country with them and then actually following through with it? Lots of memories were made with Fred and we will catch up for a beer one day to discuss the madness that was riding Vietnam.

With Fred gone, a hungover Chevs and I decided to mourn his leaving with some beers and lots of fatty food. Whilst sat outside DMZ bar we met an Australian girl named Jodie who was solo travelling like a nutter. She was double handy to talk to as she had travelled the North of Vietnam and lived in Australia, a place where we would be visiting for some time at the end of our Asian adventure. She must've got bored with us asking her questions like two annoying school children, but she seemed to like us and we arranged to go for more beers that evening at our hostel. Being a few sandwiches short of a picnic, we had also decided that we were going to get our motorbike registration plates inked onto our arms that night.

I'll skip the night out because the real madness started at just gone midnight. We stumbled out of Brown Eyes which was yet again brilliant and asked a few people where the nearest tattoo parlour was. We were informed that parlours here shut at 10:00 pm, something to do with the law, grow up! A man on his motorbike who I'm pretty sure was trying to sell drugs to people approached us and asked if we are looking for a tattoo. My head said no but my drunk mouth said yes to which he told us he had a friend who would do it for us at his house. Writing this sober and a few years later it is clear to me that we shouldn't have got on these bikes but there we were, on the back of two bikes riding to a Vietnamese drug dealer's mates house for a tattoo. It was either that or he was going to just drive us out of the town, rob us, kill us and then that would've been that. He didn't kill us else I wouldn't be writing this, although at one stage Chevs and I did discuss jumping off and legging it. We were on the bikes for a long time and ended up in rural Vietnam, there was no going back.

We arrived at this house and were greeted by an entire family who were not scary at all, they were very nice and welcoming considering we were steaming and it was the early hours of the morning. We were in too deep to reject the tattoos now so I volunteered myself to go first. They took us into a side room which contained a couch, a computer, a printer and a metal chair. It was the perfect location to kill me, chop me up and dispose of me without anyone ever knowing. All of a sudden, I was regretting saying I would go first but Chevs was comfy on the sofa with a beer in his hand by then. The tattoo artist walked through the door and I almost fell off the metal chair. This lad was 14-years-old tops, Chevs burst out laughing which made me feel even worse about the whole situation. He should have still been completing colouring books with crayons not ramming inky needles in people. I showed the infant a picture of my number plate and told him that is what I wanted. He popped it onto his computer in Times New Roman, made it slightly bigger, bolded it and looked at me for approval. 'I haven't got much choice here youngun.' I nodded.

To my amazement, 78-N1 86.55 was perfectly etched onto my left arm just above the elbow crease on my bicep. It looked considerably better than the one I had done in a professional shop in Bangkok. He wiped the blood away and wrapped me up in cling-film and I was genuinely astounded by the skill of this year 8 student. I turned around to see that Chevs was asleep on the sofa, so I slapped him awake and he got his tattoo done on his tricep just above the elbow, again an adequate job. I'm not sure if the needles were sterilised and I am certain that it was an illegal tattoo but I lived to tell the tale. We paid the young man £15 each and had to pay an extra £5 each for the transport there and back which is an absolute bargain if you ask me. Yes, I risked being robbed as well as getting a dirty needle stuck in me a contracting Aids but no risk no reward in this life, we had ended up with two good tattoos and a very good story to tell when people asked about them. We arrived back at our hostel at around 4 am and hit the hay. Unbelievably we had a full day of drinking to do shortly because it was my birthday.

Wednesday 22nd February, what year? Every year

It was my 23rd birthday and I had woken up with a new tattoo and a hangover, fantastic. The one day a year where there is no option but to say yes to beers is your birthday so when Chevs ordered me a pint with breakfast, I took a deep breath and sipped away painfully slowly. We had planned to go and visit a private beach that day with Australian Jodie, Swedish Lisa, Welsh Faye and English Holly. We had met them all the night before whilst boozing in DMZ. They enjoyed beer just as much as we did and were up for a trip to the beach followed by a shit shirt night through Hue.

Getting to the beach meant Chevs and I riding and the girls trusting us idiots with their lives which they did quite happily. I took Holly and Lisa and Chevs took Faye, Jodie's hostel was closer to the beach so she could just walk there. Lisa from Sweden was smoking hot, I was very clearly never going to get anywhere near her in a romantic/sexual way but I planned to give her my best undateable flirting.

On the way to the beach, I ran over a puppy. I realise I have just dropped that in casually but there is no other way to put it. It ran across the road, I swerved to miss it, it stopped and I ran over its head. It was, without doubt, the worst I have felt in my entire life. I would have rather ran over a human. The only silver lining was that the dog was dead on impact, Chevs confirmed this as he rode past and shouted 'Its head was the wrong way!' Not the best birthday present but we move on.

The beach was lovely and I got to see Lisa in a bikini which confirmed she was some sort of Swedish goddess. Faye, Holly and Lisa had travelled solo and met randomly and became friends! It is amazing how three people from three different countries can just meet, get along and decide to travel together. Once the sun went in and I was cooked to medium-rare we headed back to our hostels to get changed into our most rascal attire and commenced operation getting hell of a* boozy.

At the hostel that night there was a quiz on, I use quiz in the lightest of terms, it was just another excuse to get everyone drunk. You had to drink if you answered a question correctly, drink twice if you answered incorrectly and do a shot if you got the very difficult bonus question wrong. The chap doing the quiz was English and drinking along with every question so come the end was making little to no sense. The quiz master wandered over and I asked the same question I had asked everyone I had met from the UK, 'Where you from then?' He was from a place called Bromley not too far from London, I knew this because my most handsome friend Doug from Solent was born there. It's a pretty big place with a population of 330,000 so the chances of them knowing each other were slim-to-none but I was going to ask the question.

'You don't know Doug Fairbrother do you?' He looked at me as if I had just told him I had brought back his dead great grandad and he was there with me. Not only did he know Doug, but his brother was also his best mate. Backalong, in England, we had a bar crawl and Doug's mates joined, one of them was called Blue, I'll never forget his name because, well, you just wouldn't, would you? Blue was Harleys' older brother and Harley was standing in front of me as the quizmaster. A mixture of alcohol and shock left me a bit mind blown, this was the closest person to someone I knew that I had met. Harley knew me by my name, I'm not a big deal or anything like that, it was because Doug had tagged him in my Facebook post about my motorbike and said it was just like his. Mental. Harley found out it was my birthday, proceeded to get a lot more shots in and he and his Canadian girlfriend joined us for the night out. They had an ass-flavoured shot in Vietnam Backpackers and apparently, it was common for them to be consumed if it was your birthday. I had one and it tasted like someone had taken a watery shit in my mouth, a vile drink with a suitable name.

The usual route was taken, Hostel – DMZ – Brown Eyes followed by a stumble home. I loved every second of it and was very grateful that people made an effort to come out and get drunk for my birthday considering most of them had only just met me. Chevs had to come out, I would have dragged him out of an Intensive Care Unit to make sure he was there. The best birthday present would have been taking sexy Swedish Lisa back to my hostel for a minute of pure disappointment but that, as it was blatantly never going to, didn't happen. I couldn't pull a pint.

*Hell of a is an expression that I have used for a long time and it is one that doesn't make sense to me either. The sun is hell of a hot, McTominay is hell of a good at football, running is hell of a hard, you get the picture.

Thursday 23rd February 2017

This was a tough, tough day. I had woken up naked on top of my bed sheets with a room full of new people who I'm sure were less than impressed with the state of me. Chevs wasn't even in his bed and none of my new roommates had seen a massive, long-haired, human-sized baby stumbling about Hue. I wasn't worried about him though, he had a sixth sense that allowed him to make his way home no matter how blind drunk he was. I was right not to worry, I walked downstairs to the bar for some breakfast and there he was, asleep in one of the booths. You thought I was going to say still drinking, didn't you? Even Chevs has a limit it turns out.

Not a single beer was drunk as we reflected on what had been an unexpectedly great stop in Hue. I am sure thousands of people will have stopped in Hue for a day or two and thought it was the Pattaya of Vietnam, a fresh pile of slightly runny dog shit. I thought it was bloody brilliant.

Friday 24th February 2017

As we walked downstairs to check out we were greeted by Hurricane Hue outside. It was bucketing it down which wasn't ideal because we had a long ride to complete. I had some waterproofs gifted to me by the French chap who I purchased Reg from as he informed me that the North was wetter than an otter's pocket. Chevs had no such luck so he purchased a fake North Face jacket from a shop for £20, that'll do. I was already wet just from walking to the bikes so was excited to put my waterproofs on and enjoy a cosy, dry ride, I even had some wellies to slip on.

Some little twat had stolen my waterproofs. I had left them on the back of my bike in a black bag which made it look like a bag of rubbish tied down with every single bungee cord that I had. When I arrived at my bike every single bungee cord was undone and the black bag of dryness and comfort was no longer. Shit. For some reason, they had left the wellies. I popped back into the same shop Chevs had just purchased his fake North Face jacket and did the same, she had just made a quick 40 quid out of us two doughnuts.

Fun fact, fake waterproof North Face jackets are not waterproof, mine was as useful as a glass hammer. For anyone wanting to ask what my least favourite journey was during my time in Vietnam, no one ever has but just in case, it was this ride for Hue to Phong Nha. Within five minutes of riding, I was wetter than a submarine's number plate and I could feel the water seeping on to my bones. This rain was coming in sideways, directly at us as we rode through it. I was shouting and moaning in my helmet like a child the whole way there. I couldn't process how wet I was getting. At the halfway point we decided that we needed to do something about the situation else we were likely to die of hypothermia or depression, whichever took us first. We stopped in a local supermarket that didn't sell anything of real use to us so we purchased some pink washing up gloves and some plastic bags to wrap around our feet. At this stage my hands and feet had no feeling in them at all, they were completely numb and pointless. I can understand why the thief didn't steal the wellies. The accessories weren't the most fashionable but long gone was my image of being a bad-boy biker with a leather jacket. I was now riding wearing pink washing up gloves, plastic bags and a Norf Race jacket, not my best look I'll admit.

We made it to Phong Nha after just over seven hours in the seat. If the hostel that we were staying in didn't have a hot shower I was ready to go into full meltdown mode and kill everyone there followed by myself. Thankfully the hostel had a lovely hot shower and the warm water hitting my skin was pure happiness. I sat down in that shower for a good 15 minutes. There was also an extremely cute puppy at the hostel and I hugged him a lot because I still felt bad for killing one of his cousins. The main reason we had decided to do this terror journey all in one go was that we were meeting up yet again with the Pompy lot for the final leg of our Vietnam journey. This was good news for many reasons, but mainly because Alice and Tom, being the supremely efficient humans that they were, had the next week or so fully planned out for us all. I also got my medical necklace back which meant I was free to have a heart attack whenever I fancied. Laura, bless her heart, had kept the necklace safe for a good couple of weeks so I ensured I bought her Phong Na's finest beer as a thank you. Phong Nha was a relatively calm place and the only reason we were there was to visit its caves. I'd have rather missed them if I'm honest because caves are just big scary holes in the Earth that make me feel very claustrophobic, I had a bad experience in Wookey Hole as a child leaving me scarred for life.

Saturday 25th February 2017

We visited the caves that as expected made me feel like the entire world was closing in on me. Tom had rented a moped to ride to them, he was a secret biker at heart and would have loved to have ridden Vietnam, but his intelligent brain worked out that it probably wasn't worth risking his and his better half's life. The ride there consisted of steep inclines and some very poorly maintained tracks which made it quite difficult especially for everyone bar me who had two people on their bike. Call me selfish all you want I wanted an easy ride.

The caves involved a lot of walking, a lot of steps and a lot of slippery declines. It was only the last cave that we visited that was anything close to good. It was accessed by a long zip wire followed by a short kayak to the entrance. This was quite cool and it made me wish that all attractions were accessible this way, maybe I would like temples more if I could zip wire into them. I doubt it but you never know. Once we were in the cave it was pitch black and there was thick mud everywhere making it extremely difficult to walk. Only about 25% of the head torches issued by the tour company worked as well which was handy considering we were balls-deep in a pitch-black cave. The cave itself wasn't enjoyable at all; it was just a lot of shouting 'I can't see' and bumping into other people. The lake it was on was just like every other lake in the world, only considerably smaller. To make up for dragging us up to these holes in the side of a hill the tour company had erected a Total Wipeout-Esque assault course above the water which had certainly never passed a health and safety check. It was a fucking death trap.

Being competitive man-children, Chevs, Tom and I decided that we would complete this course before leaving. I often watch Total Wipeout and think I could complete it without too much difficulty, and I certainly wouldn't be as excited as those on the television are if I did! Alice and Laura accepted us for the idiots that we were and watched on hoping that they weren't about to witness any deaths. Tom went first and got about halfway before falling. I should've realised when he didn't complete it that I had no chance and not bothered, he was in much better shape than me. I went second and I swung from one obstacle onto a rope-bed and gave myself seventh-degree burns. I jumped off into the water which initially soothed my burns but then hurt them even more. Chevs proceeded to do exactly what I had just done moments before. We were now all burnt and sore.

Monday 27th February 2017

This was a sad day for Chevs and me because it was the last time that we would ride our beloved motorbikes. Despite the number of breakdowns and abuse directed their way we had grown extremely fond of them. I would miss hearing Reginald splutter into a start and being able to stop on the side of the road to take in a view or to grab some street food. Even though it hurt my back, my backside, my arms and my ears I was so happy that we bought motorbikes and didn't travel Vietnam by bus. My advice to anyone travelling Vietnam is to do so on a motorbike if you can. Even if you can't, like me, you should at least try. Please do not hold me responsible should a lorry hit you leaving your brain on the pavement.

We did play with the idea of riding the bikes into Laos and down into Thailand however, reports suggested that the roads there made Vietnam seem like a freshly paved motorway. For our last ride, we had decided to take the longer and more scenic route to Hanoi to spend an extra couple of hours on the bikes. It was certainly scenic, at one stage we were stuck in traffic behind a cow and carriage. Along the way I stopped at a barbershop and had the best cut-throat I have ever had, it was unbelievably hard to find someone in Asia that could just shave my hair off so this was a real treat.

When we eventually arrived in Hanoi we were greeted with the most traffic I have ever seen, this place made Ho Chi Minh look like a peaceful country lane. We were immediately sucked into the carnage and spat back out the other side with absolutely no idea where each other were. I aimlessly rode around Hanoi for a good hour or so getting beeped at and shunted before giving up on finding the hostel, every single street looked the same. I contacted Chevs from the WiFi of some roadside café and explained to him that he would have to come and get me because I had no idea where he or I was. Reginald was parked up outside and I ordered a very strong coffee from the slightly crazy lady in the café. I didn't panic about being lost by that stage, I just accepted it. 20 Minutes later, Chevs and Laura came around the corner to save me, by this time I was bouncing off the walls because the coffee that crazy lady had made me was pure caffeine. Chevs had parked his bike up in a local car park already and had to direct me to where it was. I retained zero of the instructions he gave to me so I asked if he would just jump on the back of my bike and take me there. Oversized human on the back we made the short trip to the car park and I parked Reginald up for the last time. A couple of pictures later and both bikes were listed on Vietnam's version of Auto-Trader and every Facebook page possible. It was basically Tinder for bikes, you'd scroll until you found the one you like and then message the owner asking for a ride. There was immediate interest from people in our two utterly crap motorbikes, interest that would have to wait because we were off to Halong Bay which involved a 5 am bus. Time to get our nuts down.

Tuesday 28th February 2017

Our nights' sleep was interrupted by a girl in our room having the hinges blown off of her by a grunting American man. No matter how many times Alice coughed they weren't stopping, someone could've jammed a knife in his back and he would've kept pumping away. This was my first experience of people shagging in the same room as me, well, that I can remember, most of the time I was in a beer induced coma. Eventually, after what seemed like an eternity there was a final moan followed by a final grunt and I could sleep peacefully. We all ensured to make as much noise as possible when we woke up at 4:30 am for our 5 am bus. I developed a very loud sneeze overnight and really couldn't keep it in on multiple occasions. The two lovers didn't budge, they were very tired out.

The 5 am bus was as subdued as you would expect, everyone was shattered and in no mood for talking. I dozed off almost immediately only to be awoken by Chevs tapping me moments later. 'Stringer has just got on the bus with Lauren.' He said to me like an excited puppy dog. Stringer and Lauren were two people we knew from university, we had worked with Stringer at Café Parfait nightclub being the tossers offering you deals to come into the nightclub and I may or may not have had sexual relations with one of Laurens housemates. How we know them doesn't matter, we know them. I told Chevs that he needed to get some sleep because there was no chance that they had just walked on the same bus as us and were coming to Halong Bay. I looked forward at the two culprits and could only see the back of their heads. Ok, they had the same colour hair as them but how many brown-haired men and blonde-haired women travelled together? I'm guessing billions.

I dozed back off until we arrived at the boat named Castaways that we would be cruising around Halong Bay on, it was nothing special, if anything it was a bit budget, but it would do. We weren't sleeping on the boat, we had a hostel on dry land which we would be staying in which suited me perfectly as I didn't like the idea of sleeping on a boat at sea. As we walked off the bus Stringer turned around and looked straight at us, fair enough Benjamin you were right on this occasion. We couldn't believe that they were all on the same boat tour. We were travelling in completely different directions at different times yet somehow, we both ended up on the same tour of 32 people in Halong Bay. It was great to see some familiar faces, Stringer and Lauren were another exceptionally attractive couple, similar to Tom and Al only Solent educated and therefore dopier. One thing that they could do was drink, Solent prepares you well for that and that is exactly what we would be doing for the next two days.

The boat took us through Halong Bay which was like something off of a movie. It has probably been in a movie. I'd be very surprised if David Attenborough hasn't been on the TV there before. Halfway through the trip our elected Tour Guide / Team-Leading drunk human, Nina, stopped the boat and told us that we would all be going kayaking for a couple of miles around some of the smaller islands. I would have rather stayed on the top deck having a drink but this kayaking was non-negotiable. I hopped in with Tom and ensured that we had enough beer to see us through the next two hours or so of kayaking. I'm not sure I helped much in the rowing department, but I did hand Tom beer or three and drank plenty myself, all in all, it was a very nice way to spend an afternoon. Back on the boat we continued to drink and with drink came introductions to different people that we would be sharing a 32-bed-dorm room with. Here's a whistle-stop tour of who we met.

Eric, he was a scouser that loved football and boozing. Young, he was an Asian-American who had a drone. Lizzie, she fancied Asian men. Rosie, she liked tequila and Mexican food. Chris, he was a proper traveller, indulged in culture, took some great photographs and did not have dreadlocks. There was more but there are only so many faces and people my brain can remember. We will just assume they were all boring.

We arrived back on dry land and were all reasonably trollied. We made the short walk past the lovely resort that was on the island and walked towards our prison-chic dorm. The owner had stuck some fancy basins and left us with a nice view to look at as we washed our hands and brushed our teeth but there was no doubt this was a hell hole. This would matter very little to me as I would only use the room for sleeping in, the rest of my time would be spent in the bar below boshing alcoholic beverages. It didn't take long for things to get out of hand, the bar was a bring your own booze establishment and luckily we had overstocked. Everyone had bottles of spirits which the tour website clearly stated not to bring and we proceeded to make some mental cocktails that blew our heads off. Tom ended up so shit-faced that he puked all over the sinks, therefore, ruining the only half-decent thing about the hostel. 'What a lovely view to be sick in front of.' Tom groaned as he curled up in a ball on the floor. It was hard to argue with that fact.

Wednesday 1st March 2017

The energy was at an all-time low that morning. Everyone in the room was moaning, groaning and debating whether it was worth doing day two of the trip. Nina bustled in all bright-eyed and bushy-tailed despite drinking with us until the early hours and told us to get ready and be at breakfast within the hour, she was a professional at this. This may seem like a realistic time scale but there were only two showers for 32 people and Toms sick occupied one of the three sinks. I know it's not hygienic, but I sacked off the shower and just dragged myself down for some breakfast. It was a massive buffet of all the things that I love, mainly bacon and hash browns. I indulged and felt on the verge of being human again, more than could be said for Tom who had the handbrake up on struggle street.

For some unknown reason, the day's activities included a bike ride on another island, what kind of sick individual created this tour? Exercise was lower on my to-do list than gauging my eyes out with a rusty spoon, yet that is what I did and it was horrific. The bikes that we were given were single-speed thigh destroyers made in the early '90s. Every single pedal hurt and as soon as there was any kind of incline, we were all off and pushing. Ok, it was just me off and pushing. This was not my idea of fun. The island we cycled around was lovely but not much different to ours, maybe a little bit bigger. I preferred our island because it had rum and a bed.

As Nina wanted to kill us all we then got off of the bikes and went on a trek up a mountain that was not fit for climbing. The only reason we took this hike was so we could go and see the monkeys that lived on the beach on the other side. This pleased Chevs as he had longed to see a monkey. Back when we were on the island off of Shitaya in Thailand we visited a beach named 'Monkey Beach' which was home to all of zero monkeys. Even they were sick of the place. We arrived and from a distance, they were quite cute but as soon as you got close they would try and rip your throat out, vicious little things. Nina's day two tour sucked and I told her on multiple occasions, get us back to our island.

Once back on the island we were informed that we would be eating in the fancy resort for the evening, the posh were going to let the peasants in, how very kind of them. They had probably spent thousands on their nice trip to Halong bay so were understandably annoyed to see a group of smelly backpackers turn up and eat all of their food. The food was out of this world, they had the freshest muscles I have ever eaten and some chocolate dessert that put me into a food coma. That night we got suitably drunk although Tom was consuming at a much, much slower pace.

I've never heard anyone say a bad word about Halong Bay. Despite the bike ride and the death hike, I was incredibly impressed by this place. Whether you are with your mates, girlfriend, family or just on your own like a psychopath this place is a must-visit. It's pretty close to paradise

Thursday 2nd March 2017
Initially, the plan was for everyone from the trip to go out that evening but the majority bailed on us, however, three die-hard Solent alumni managed to dust off the cobwebs and head to some local bars. Stringer, Chevs and I weren't about to be defeated by a boat tour of Halong Bay, we'd completed two weeks of Freshers in our pomp.

We were involved in a lock-in at the bar we had based ourselves at. Back home I love nothing more than a lock-in at The Armoury. The old Landlord Martin would shut his doors and end up drunker than any of us still drinking in his pub often getting naked. I was hopeful that this lock-in ended up 50% as mad as those back home. Little did we know that the police patrolled the streets of Hanoi and all the bars had to be closed with no customers inside after midnight. This was disappointing news as I assumed that would put an end to our late lock-in plans. Thankfully, there was a simple and effective way bars could avoid this whilst breaking the law in the process, pulling the shutters down, turning the music lower and continuing to serve alcohol to those inside.

The bar also served up balloons which were said to give a 15 second high. I had never had one before so thought this would be as good a time as any to try one, so I took a balloon, put it in my mouth and inhaled and exhaled for 30 seconds. Everything went a bit blurry and everyone's voices went into slo-mo which was strange. As I blinked myself back into focus I noticed that Stringer had a bleeding nose, my instant thought was that he was dying. I have seen enough Netflix crime documentaries to know that bleeding from the nose is never a good sign. The reason was much less serious, he had face-planted the bar whilst inhaling his balloon, sucked it too hard!

We left the bar at just gone 2 am and snuck in some street food on the way home. I fell into bed fully clothed and was asleep as soon as my head hit the pillow. I was the sort of boozy and tired that only normally happens at Christmas after too much turkey.

Friday 3rd March 2017

The day had finally come to wave goodbye to our bikes. We had completed over 1400 miles on the old Honda's and they were ready to do it all over again with some other backsides sitting on them. We had received a lot of interest in the two bikes advertised for 275 American Dollars and were off to meet a couple of Americans that Rosie the tequila lover from Halong Bay had pointed in our direction. They had both ridden bikes before, bikes that were in much better condition and much more powerful than ours. In fairness, our bikes were in pretty good shape, we had each had a fair amount of work done on them during our trip up. We knew $275 was asking for too much but we wanted to sell them for as close to $250 as possible, wheeler-dealers and all that. They haggled us down to a very fair $225 and as soon as the money was in my bank I handed over my helmet and keys. There's no paperwork involved with these bike sales, nor is there any insurance documents or tax. I'm not sure how legal the whole process is, all I know is that thousands of tourist's bike Vietnam every year and I don't think many get pulled over for not having tax and insurance. Looking back, it is probably very illegal.

For the rest of that day, we mourned our bikes and wandered around Hanoi which was a crazy city with far too many humans and motorbikes. It was anti-socially busy and impossible to walk and talk without getting bumped into. We met up with Rosie and Liz for tequila and Mexican because we owed Rosie a drink for sourcing the buyers, not bad commission.

We kept in touch with the two Americans that bought our bikes for a while. Dustin was very open and honest with me about his experience on my motorbike and informed me that it was, and I quote, 'Fucking awful.'

Another night bus was awaiting us at 9 pm, this time to Sapa, a place high in the sky in the North of Vietnam. It was a game of potluck visiting this place if you got good weather it was said to be one of the best places in Vietnam and if it was bad weather it was going to be a complete waste of time. It seemed a bit of an unnecessary gamble to me. The bus that arrived back from Sapa just before we left told us that they couldn't see two feet in front of them let alone the views which was not what we wanted to hear. Review listened too and dismissed Chevs and I jumped on the bus with the Pompy lot. Alice had organised this for us as well, she was a good egg.

This night bus was slightly more bearable than the Virak Buntham express in Cambodia, everyone had their own seat-cum-bed that was relatively comfortable for an hour and then impossible to get comfortable in The idea of a night bus was to sleep through the journey, so when I arrived I was set to be refreshed and where I needed to be.

Saturday 4th March 2017

When we arrived in Sapa I was exhausted and in a place that was far colder than I had expected it to be. The good news was that the weather was clear and you could see for miles over the rice-field-mountain things which Chevs eloquently described as 'alright.' We popped into a hotel where our tour guides came and retrieved us to take us on a trek to our host house. I popped over the road to a street stall that was selling warm socks and hats. A great example of supply and demand, this woman was making a mint out of underprepared travellers like me. I still have the hat to this day, bright orange and if anything, it makes me too hot.

The trek across to our host-house was quite difficult, this should have been expected considering we were up a mountain, but I imagined it to be more of a stroll. There wasn't a whole lot happening in Sapa, the rice fields were impressive, and the views were a bit more than alright, but it wasn't amazing. When we arrived at the host house it became clear that it was going to be a waste of time. We were in a house with a host family who wanted nothing to do with us or the 15 other people we had never met before. We made the most out of an average situation and had a slight detox whilst we were in the hills of Sapa. The host family cooked us some very good food which suggested that maybe that didn't mind us after all although there were a couple of cocky young French lads that everyone minded, they were a pair of annoying pricks. They told of how they were elite athletes back in France and went out for runs throughout the day, if only they had run straight off the top of the mountain.

It didn't matter if the host family liked us or not, somehow they had the Manchester United game on their TV and we were watching it even if it meant sitting on their laps. It turned out that they liked us more when they found out a couple of us were United fans. The universal language of football. Tom and I sat in their lounge with the whole family watching Manchester United and snacking on the nuts that they had on the table.

There is no sugarcoating day two of Sapa, it wasn't any good. It was no different than day one only the trek was steeper and more difficult.

Wednesday 8th March 2017

My time in Vietnam was coming to an end and there were only two things left to do, say goodbye and get very drunk with The Pompy lot and a few others. In Hanoi some people have large kegs of beer and sell them outside on street corners, they will have plastic chairs, plastic cups and be willing to serve you a pint for as little as 15 pence, the cheapest I found anywhere in Asia. When the beer is 15 pence it doesn't take very long or very much to get drunk, a couple of quid later everyone that was around the table with us was seeing double. Chris from Halong got involved and we were also joined by some locals who were having a great laugh. They took great pleasure in seeing us struggling to talk after far too many beverages. One of my favourite photos from my travels was taken that night. A table half filled with backpackers and the other half filled with locals all absolutely steaming and having a great time. The night ended with me on Chevs' shoulders in a makeshift street party which involved a few of the street bars. A fitting end!

We had to say our goodbyes to Alice, Tom and Laura who would be going their separate ways, Tom and Al to Thailand and Laura back home to the UK. They had played a big part in our journey and were incredibly patient with the two airheads that are Chevs and I. It was only a goodbye for now though, when possible I was certain that we would meet again, as long as Alice organised it.

There were no mixed feelings about leaving Vietnam, I was outright depressed about it. I had loved the last month of riding through this unexpectedly beautiful country whose people were the kindest I have ever met. I doubt I will ever recommend a country so highly to visit, it was extraordinary. I will offer one piece of advice which you can save for a rainy day, get the three-month Visa if you can, I wish I had.

Laos

Thursday 9th March 2017

As if I wasn't depressed enough about leaving Vietnam, I was doing so on a 24-hour sleeper bus to Luang Prabang, Laos. Chevs, the most positive human I have ever met, was equally as depressed about the thought of this, some form of joint suicide was on the horizon. Hindsight is a wonderful thing, but why we never just paid the extra money to get a flight across absolutely baffles me. It would've been the best money I had spent as well because this 24 hours on a bus was relentless torture.

The bus itself was small and cramped which meant it was impossible to get comfortable on the leather seats-cum-beds. It was also the same temperature as the earth's core, so I was getting stuck to the seats-cum-beds because I was sweating like a dyslexic on Countdown. There were no charging points on the bus either so a couple of episodes of Vikings in my phone had run out of battery which meant I had nothing to do. I had no book, no tablet, no laptop, just my thoughts for 22 hours. Add to this that the bus driver was a maniac and you have yourself a mental asylum on wheels. At one stage I was sat up with my arms hugging my knees rocking like someone in need of an exorcism. It was without question the worst 24 hours I have ever experienced.

I lost track of time and days and didn't know who I was anymore, but we made it to Laos in one piece physically. Mentally, I was shot to bits.

Saturday 11th March 2017

Good Morning Luang Prabang! It doesn't have the same ring to it, does it? This place sucked and it sucked real bad! Our hostel was full of those plonkers who had found themselves on their travels and those who were travelling on Daddy's money. They couldn't be further away from the sort of people I wanted to spend any time with, I had no interest in finding out about their meditation techniques nor the rug they'd knitted.

Luang Prabang can be described in a sentence. It has a nice waterfall and a bowling alley that you can go and get drunk at after the curfew. That's that. We move on.

Tuesday 14th March 2017

We escaped tosser-traveller central and made our way down to Vang Vieng. This was another place that was undoubtedly going to have very little about it but there was the infamous tubing to take part in. Tubing in Vang Vieng consists of getting a rubber dingy and going on a pub crawl along the Mekong river. Backalong, this used to attract thousands of travellers and it would be the party of a lifetime! Tragically, lots of travellers have lost their lives on these boozy, drug-fuelled bar crawls down a fast-flowing river which resulted in the government cracking down, understandable. They still did the bar crawls although they were said to be a lot more above board and safe nowadays with only a couple of bars to stop at.

Tuesday was the day that all of the bar staff and workers would go on the bar crawl and was said to be the liveliest of any day to grab a tube and get wild on the Mekong. As chance would have it we would be doing it on a Tuesday. Chevs promised me that he hadn't planned for this, I did not believe him. It was lively but not the Project X level lively that it had become famous for. There was plenty of alcohol getting drunk and lots of drinking games getting played which made it a good day out. We ended up chatting to plenty of people, some of which had been working in Vang Vieng for over three months, strange humans. Those that were just travelling through all had the same view on Laos, it was below average. This was good to hear because we wouldn't be spending very long in Laos at all.

Getting the tube to the pick-up point at the end of the crawl was quite difficult after a few beers, I could see how people had died on this trip, the river's current was seriously fast! If you had been on the happy mushrooms or anything similar and weren't completely with it you wouldn't stand much of a chance if you came off the dingy. As I jumped off my ring and put my feet on the bottom of the river it took me by surprise and I slipped and lost both of my sliders that I was wearing. This was gutting because they were perfectly moulded to my feet by then and I knew that the next sliders I bought would give me blisters instantly. Rather them floating down the Mekong than me though.

With tubing survived and enjoyed we continued to get drunk at the Irish bar in Vang Vieng and then stumbled into the local nightclub. On the walk home, we disagreed on the direction we were walking. As he is much bigger than me he got his own way but I moaned and let him know that he was wrong. I told him he was wrong almost constantly until we arrived at our hostel. He didn't say a word, smug prick.

Thursday 16th March 2017

We arrived in Don Det which was yet another nothing place. Some lad was wearing a t-shirt with 'Been There, Don Det' printed on the front which made me want to throw a rock at his head. It had it's positives though, we would be meeting Liz and Rosie from Halong Bay fun times and Sean and Nicole from Bangkok bedlam. We had advised them all in advance that we were here for a detox, no beers at all.

We stuck to our guns but when we met Rosie and Liz that night we indulged in a *magic cookie* which was said to have some marijuana in it. I didn't mind the idea of this, getting lightly baked with some friends and undoubtedly ending up talking shite and eating loads. Now I'm not sure what was actually in this cookie, if I had to guess I would say there was some form of hallucinogenic in them, it was not just weed that is for sure. I ate half and after 20 minutes nothing happened. Rosie was having a little moment and the cookies were making her slightly loopy in the head. Chevs and I thought bollocks to these stupid £5 cookies so ate the remaining halves and started to walk home. Then it hit me, like a Mike Tyson right hook straight on my bonce.

I looked out at the sea view and saw lightning coming from the sky. Bearing in mind the weather forecast was clear as it could be and there was zero chance of thunder and lightning, I was seeing huge forks crashing into the sea. There were biblical scenes in my frazzled mind. As we got home things took a peculiar turn and a stray dog took a bite out of my leg. I was led in my bed on the bottom bunk rocking like a lunatic whispering up to Chevs on the top bunk that I had been bitten by a stray dog. Clear as day I could see the dog outside the room taunting me and the bleeding gash in my leg. 'I'm going to fucking die, I'm going to die of fucking rabies. CHEVS!' We were both useless to each other at this stage, Chevs was on his trip and wasn't enjoying it one bit either. He regularly informed me that he could not move. At least he hadn't been bitten by a stray.

All of a sudden, I started feeling extremely sick, my mind blamed it on rabies that I had just contracted. I couldn't go outside as the dog was there, I couldn't be sick on my bed because I had to sleep there tomorrow night. I had no choice but to be brave and leave the room. I stood up and shouted at the dog whilst moving exceptionally slowly. The dog scurried and I walked outside the room and puked in the bin. This made me feel a lot better, but I was still worried the dog would come back and maul me to death, so I went back to bed ensuring that the door was shut firmly behind me. Thankfully the dog never came back to finish me off.

When I woke the next morning, I had a t-shirt tied around my calf which I removed to find absolutely nothing. There was no bite, there was no stray dog, I was tripping out of my brain the whole time. The people of the hostel looked at me like I was an insane person which was completely fair enough, I wouldn't be making any friends here and I certainly wouldn't be eating any cookies again, good god no.

Friday 17th March 2017

I may not have made any friends in Don Det but Chevs had, he had taken a liking to a Canadian named Arya. Chevs had spent the entire day talking to Arya in a bid to win her love, he only had 24 hours as we would be leaving for Thailand then. The clock was ticking. We went for dinner with Arya and her friend Sansa and had also arranged to meet Sean and Nicole. I'm almost certain Sean wouldn't have remembered bumping into us, he had chowed down on one of the cookies and was midway through a head loss when we saw him. Nicole was as nice as always, but our reunion was short-lived, it was good to see that Sean hadn't changed though, what a guy!

Chevs failed to seduce Arya over dinner and I advised Sansa not to eat any cookies. Don Det came to an end with me led in a dorm full of people that thought I was a prick. Been there, Don Det.

Saturday 18th March 2017

I see your sleeper bus and I raise you a sleeper train. I can't express to you how much better this mode of transport is compared to the death buses. The sleeper train took us from Laos back to Bangkok in Thailand. We weren't mental and going back for round two with Khao San Road nor were we going to buy a suit because we regretted not owning one in 34-degree heat. We were only in Bangkok to catch a plane to Chiang Mai in the North. The 24-hour bus into Laos had officially put us off of travelling overnight by bus again so from then on we would travel on trains, boats and aeroplanes with the occasional day bus for short journeys. There was no drama at all on this night train, it was comfortable, quiet and had charging ports.

We arrived in Bangkok and didn't have to stay for very long before jumping on the plane to Chiang Mai. I was hopeful that Thailand, like Vietnam, was better up North. We wouldn't find out until a day or so later because all in all the sleeper train and plane took us well over 24 hours including some delays. Once we arrived on the 19th at 9 pm it was time to hit the hay in a hostel that was an absolute dream! We had a six-bed dorm to ourselves, the beds had memory foam mattresses and the air-conditioning was hell of a chilly.

Thailand, The Return of The Dingers

Tuesday 21st March 2017

Throughout our travels Chevs and I had discussed visiting elephants on a few occasions however, we had never got around to doing so. We usually opted for an all-dayer instead. One of these discussions happened in Pattaya where I am pretty sure the elephants would've been donkeys with a toilet roll tube glued on their nose. We had waited until Chiang Mai as they had elephant sanctuaries, a place where rescued elephants would go to live a happy life and not get chained up and rode by stupid tourists. If you have ever ridden an elephant or plan on riding one in the future then you are a crap human. If you were wondering how much Chevs likes elephants, don't forget he has a tattoo of one on his back, he was very excited!

The sanctuary was only a short bus ride away and it was worth the wait! Huge elephants were roaming around in complete freedom. Those who worked there dedicated their lives to guard these animals and ensure they were safe from poachers and circuses. If you have ever shot an elephant then please use this book to light a fire, wait until it's big and jump straight into that fire. There was an element of fear involved as the elephants were humongous, if they wanted to charge us they would have just trampled us to death within seconds. Thankfully they didn't do this to anyone on our trip and we were able to spend a few hours with the elephants, feeding them and then joining them in a mud bath. There was a baby elephant there that was very similar to a puppy dog only much bigger. The workers would shout its name to tell it off for misbehaving and it would disappear behind its mother like a spoilt child. Fascinating animals and ones that deserve so much better than to be hunted for their tusks.

Wednesday 22nd March 2017

Day two of doing actual traveller stuff, had we finally worked out how to do this? We hopped on another bus and headed for The White Temple in Chiang Rai. No prizes for guessing what this place was and no bonus points if you can figure out what my thoughts on it were. That's right, it was a crap white temple. No points or prizes to anyone.

After somehow spending an hour at this chavvy temple we moved on to visit the Long Neck Karen tribe, now this was a place to remember. To my surprise, this was not a tribe of women named Karen wanting to talk to the manager. You may have seen the Long Neck Karen tribe on a documentary before, they are the people that wear rings around their necks to stretch them out giving them, you got it, long necks. I met the woman who had the most rings, 30, and I have never seen anything like it, I was amazed at how the human body was able to do this without her head popping off like a dandelion. 'Is it just the neck that you can stretch with rings or would they work elsewhere on the body?' I asked her. I didn't get a response, she didn't get my banter. I popped a photo of me and the world record holder on social media and Alice replied, 'how does she fold towels?' That is all I've been able to think about since.

This busy day out meant that Chevs and I were pretty thirsty come the end of it so decided it was about time to go for a few beers in Chiang Mai. It wasn't too bad at all, it remained relatively quiet throughout which meant no queuing to get a beer, my favourite. We ended up going to the local nightclub which was an absolute travesty of a place. They had a live band playing who were seemingly Thailand's answer to Little Mix only considerably worse. An hour or so of their screaming was enough for me to tap out and head back to the hostel. Chiang Mai wasn't a place for a mad one I concluded.

Thursday 23rd March 2017

Hangover free, Chevs had booked us into yet another activity that didn't involve boozing all day. Chevs and I had to have a quick discussion to make sure we hadn't found ourselves or became very boring. I knew Chevs would never be boring, but I had to double-check that he was ok. He had booked us in for a traditional Thai cooking class for the day which I was less than impressed with, I am beyond bad at cooking. When I arrived at university, I made beans for the first time and my flatmate informed me that I had to sieve the beans once they were cooked to get rid of the bad minerals. I proceeded to sieve the beans and had the driest beans on toast in history. That's my level of cheffing. Yet there I was, picking up fresh ingredients from a local market to go and cook for myself and then eat it.

I couldn't tell you what we made for a starter, but I can remember it tasting plain. Chevs's dish was delightful so that was my bad. Dish two was a Pad Thai, something that I had grown to love during my travels. I tried hard and listened to every instruction that was given to me on this occasion, I gave this dish passion and love and it still tasted crap. Yet again Chevs had whipped up a storm and it tasted lovely! Right, third-time lucky Chef Bouch, don't waste a day! For dessert we made fried bananas which I also loved and if I managed to cock this up, I was calling an end to my cheffing career after dry beans on toast and a below-par three-course Thai. Even I managed to make these edible, they were very nice, I would say better than Chevs's but who am I to judge? Just the right amount of cinnamon and fried to perfection, bone apple tea! The instructor gave us all the recipes to use in the future which I put straight in the bin outside. I haven't cooked Thai food since, probably for the best.

Friday 24th March 2017

Our time in Chiang Mai had come to an end and we were off to Pai, a place that I had heard very good things about. I had wanted to get back on a motorbike since leaving Vietnam and the road from Chiang Mai to Pai was the perfect opportunity to do just that! Sadly, for us, the rental place didn't have any bikes, only mopeds so they had to do. I was pleasantly surprised by my twist-and-go, it was considerably faster than my motorbike although so was a light jog. Lots of travellers had crashed on this road previously so we ensured to take extra precaution even though I felt like Valentino Rossi on a bike by then. The ride took us through the winding mountains of the North and we stopped on a couple of occasions to take in the views that were riding past. It was better than Sapa that's for sure.

Once we arrived in Pai we went immediately to our hostel which was nothing more than a building site. It was like someone had started building a hostel, ran out of money and just opened it up anyway. The accommodation was terrible but the location and everything else was brilliant, they had spent their money on the land and the bar which suited me. They also had a full-size snooker table which was very obscure, I gave Chevs a game and we were both equally as bad, snooker is much more difficult than pool, we called the game at 8-5 to Chevs, a thriller. With newfound respect for Ronnie O'Sullivan, I said to Chevs it was about time we had a cold one so we headed down to the bar. They had a table tennis table which is much more my game, Chevs didn't beat me once. We also noticed pretty quickly that everyone at the bar was away with the fairies, happy enough but stoned out of their minds!

We walked into town which was a deceptively long walk and were greeted with bars galore. Every bar was full to the brim with hippies which was not surprising. This place catered for those who didn't eat meat, said yah instead of yes and, of course, had dreadlocks. Each to their own, they probably looked at me and thought what a plain, bald bastard. We found it incredibly easy to end up on a bar crawl that night, every time we left one bar we would stumble into the next and there is only one way that ends, drunkenly.

Saturday 25th March 2017

Waking up in a building site for a hostel was a strange feeling. Our dorm was a windowless room with 12 mattresses on the floor and no one seemed bothered by this at all. In fairness, the floor-mattress wasn't as uncomfortable as it looked. I went downstairs for some breakfast which I was certain was going to be foul, but I was starving. What they served up to me was the best eggs benedict I have ever had the pleasure of putting in my mouth. The hollandaise sauce made me do a little dance! A very nice surprise on a Saturday morning.

Chevs woke up a few hours later looking like shit and we decided to head to the local swimming pool for a tan top-up and recover. The local swimming pool was a pretty decent spot, it was packed out with people and had Fanta Fruit Twist in a can which is my favourite drink on a hangover. We set up camp and settled in for a well-earned sun-burning session. Twenty minutes or so into poolside and burn two Irish girls came over and asked if they could join, the most worrying thing about this was that they knew us but we didn't have a clue who they were. Maybe we had become travel famous, maybe I'd look on my YouTube to find that thousands had subscribed to me overnight and I had gone viral. I checked, still only 21 subscribers to my utterly crap vlogs. It turned out we had bumped into them the night before and they remembered talking to us because of the tattoos of our bike registrations, I knew they would be good for something! We reminisced on our meet at the bar and it all came flooding back, beer once again had transformed me into a blind man.

We sat and chatted with Stacey and Vanessa, they could talk for Ireland! By the end of the day, I knew about their families, their jobs and what their perfect Sunday consisted of. Another thing we found out was that they liked drinking so we asked if they would like to go for round two that evening to which they agreed. We went back to the hostel, got changed and did it all again only this time I remembered everything and only got blurry not blind. Can I shock you? We didn't pull that night either. What I did do was get Chevs what I owed him, his name tattooed on my body. We strolled into a tattoo parlour and I asked for Chevs to be inked on my foot for the rest of my life which they did with pleasure. I FaceTimed my little sister whilst mid-tattoo, she advised me to stop but I completely ignored her. The memories flood back when I look at the tattoo, it is one of my favourites.

Sunday 26th March 2017

The small world that is, the world, meant that a chap that used to work in the same pub as Chevs in Southampton was in Pai at the same time as us. He had contacted Ben through Facebook the day before and we had agreed to go and meet him at his hostel that day. Before we did that we had to visit Pai Canyon which is like the Grand Canyon in America only considerably shitter. We walked around the canyon that was only slightly larger than the average pothole for an hour or so and decided that it was as pointless a trip as we were ever likely to make. We got back on the mopeds and rode off to meet Tom.

Tom was staying in the Pai Circus Hostel which I assumed was just the usual funny name for a hostel, it wasn't, it was a bloody circus up there. On arrival people were juggling fire, doing backflips, bending themselves all over the place and those who had absolutely no talent at all were walking over a bit of rope between two poles. Tom wasn't a circus act himself, he was, in fact, a very normal bloke who had somehow ended up in this bonkers hostel. A couple of his mates came across and introduced themselves to us and I genuinely didn't understand what one of them said to us. He was so rah, travelled yah, found myself yah it hurt my head. But to keep Chevs happy and to allow him to spend some time with Tom I sucked up the rah and we agreed to go for some dinner with them.

Now the next part shocked me, it made me whisper to myself in disbelief 'what the fuck have I just witnessed?' I have seen a ping-pong show so I'm pretty immune to weird stuff now.

One of Toms circus friends was too deep in the traveller lifestyle. His clothes were dirty, his trousers were animal printed and he stunk like a man who hadn't had a shower for a decade. He openly admitted he hadn't washed his hair for a few months which went quite a long way to explaining why he smelt like an overflowing food bin. Anyway, Bart (I feel like I need to tell you that is not his real name because travellers like this are more than capable of changing their name to a Simpsons character) didn't have anything to eat at dinner and just chatted fodder and watched us demolish plates of Thai food which was insanely good! We then left the street-food place and Bart proceeded to put his hands into the bins on the side of the street and pull out half-eaten bits of food. My head fell clean off and was on the road. What the fuck was this guy about? I checked to make sure that he wasn't poor or mentally ill and that was not the case, he was just a complete wrongun. Stop balancing on ropes and eating out of bins please, whoever you are and I am sure there is more than one culprit, stop it, you're someone's child, have some respect.

Tuesday 28th March 2017

For unknown reasons I wanted a bamboo tattoo done in Pai. Our time in Thailand was running out rapidly and this was the ideal place to get one. The first tattoo parlour we walked past I asked if they would do me a bamboo tattoo and they agreed to it. I requested the Pi symbol on my left shoulder, witty innit?

There was instant regret as soon as he hammered the first bit of sharp bamboo into my arm and there was nothing but pain for the next hour. The tattoo artist was banging this spear so hard into my arm that it wouldn't have shocked me if he smashed it right through me and out of the other side. The result was my least favourite tattoo on my whole body, it is a lot bigger than I wanted it, but it holds a story so it is there to stay. Chevs turned down the opportunity for a bamboo tattoo once he saw my reaction, that and he was running out of skin to tattoo.

Rubbish tattoo wrapped up, we went to visit Pai hot springs later that afternoon and it was nothing short of shit. I should have taken some shower gel up with me and had a bath to make it worthwhile, Bart certainly should!

Our final night in Pai was spent with people that I genuinely had no time for as well as Chevs and Tom. We ate dinner at a lovely restaurant which cost us about £2 per person yet shockingly Bart would still rather eat from the bins the tosser. Our time in Pai had come to an end and despite staying in a building site and meeting a load of 'rah' speaking wankers I enjoyed the place. Maybe if I had stayed a bit longer I could've returned home walking across some rope a metre above the ground and ravaging through next door's food bin!

On the ride from Pai to Chiang Mai Chevs got pulled over by the police and forced pay a fine of £25 for riding without a licence. This was fair and what should have happened is he shouldn't have been allowed back on his bike because it was illegal. But the policeman let him get back on the bike and ride back to our hostel. This confused me. Chevs had been caught whilst breaking the law and then just left to continue to do it again moments later. No points on the licence, nothing, just a fine. That screams corruption if you ask me.

Saturday 1st April 2017

We had spent a few days travelling back to the South of Thailand as we had planned to visit two islands, Koh Samui and Koh Phangan. These islands were our last little taste of paradise before our South East Asia adventure came to an end. I was very excited for some care-free tanning again, it had been a while since we had just stopped and relaxed on a sun-lounger at the beach. Making this trip even more worthwhile was the fact that we would be meeting Tom and Alice on Koh Samui followed by Stringer and Lauren on Koh Phangan a few days later.

Koh Samui was exactly what we had hoped for. We stayed in the same hostel as Tom and Al, obviously Al booked it for us. The beds were little pods with a curtain at the end so it was complete privacy which meant I could sleep naked. It had a pool 10 metres back from the beach and endless amounts of sun-loungers for doing absolutely nothing on. The little island didn't have a whole lot going on, it had a strip of bars, but the main nightlife was a taxi-ride away, enough to ensure that we stayed clear of boozing. We laid in the sun all day and I fully recharged my battery which was running at around 3%. I also managed to get very sunburnt as a side effect of sitting in 35-degree sunshine all day, I was only a set of horns away from a very good Satan fancy dress costume, my head was extremely red!

This was officially goodbye-for-now to Tom and Al, they had put up with a pair of useless idiots for about three weeks of their travelling lives and we had become good friends. They were well organised and if it weren't for them we would probably be stuck on a 13-day-bender in Hoi An and handing out leaflets for Mr Beans bar. The reason we got on so well is that despite being well organised and sensible when needed, they also both knew how to let their hair down and have a laugh which is exactly how we ended up in a taxi to the bars and clubs of Koh Samui that night. We had only gone for dinner, it ended up in buckets on the beach.

A short and sweet farewell to Mr and Mrs South East Asia 2017. They would return home and have proper haircuts, wear nicer clothes and become an even more dreamy couple.

Sunday 2nd April 2017

A short trip across the water via a tiny boat and we were in Koh Phangan, a smaller and livelier island. This was where backpackers came to have a right good look at lots of beer and pills. We checked into our hostel and it had a full-size 4g football pitch behind it. This meant that every bloke spent their days booting a ball about and playing heads a volleys which was great although I struggled to head the ball due to it being a sunburnt, sore, peeling mess.

The one thing that stood out like a sore thumb in Koh Phangan was an old English pub named The Masons Arms. An English couple from Portsmouth had moved over to the island and built a pub that resembled their local back home. It brought a tear to my eye, it was the most beautiful thing I had seen in all my travels, significantly better than any temple or waterfall. Inside it was fully kitted out with old British pub décor, it even smelt like an English pub, reeking of stale beer, body odour and cigarettes. Completing the pub was wooden chairs, bar stools, a shitty old pool table and as British a menu as you could hope for in Thailand. Chevs and I were in dreamland. I had their roast dinner which was, on reflection, bang average, but at the time I can remember just groaning and mmm'ing the whole way through it. Do you have any idea how good a Yorkshire pudding filled with gravy tastes after three months of rice and noodles?

Tuesday 4th April 2017

Stringer and Lauren arrived at just the right time, there was a half-moon party taking place that night. I had heard of full moon parties but apparently, they celebrated the half just as hard! Any excuse to have a party and take more of my money. Most whatever moon it is parties consist of going to the local beach and partying until the early hours with live DJ sets and those skipping ropes that are on fire that people jump through. Everyone in the hostel and every other hostel on the island were on the beers from the early afternoon, people were painting their faces and sticking on the most outrageous clothes that they had in their backpacks. I painted my bald, peeling head and got fully indulged in the party spirit.

Lauren ordered the first shot of tequila at 4 pm which resulted in us buying shots with every round, something that was never going to end well. Luckily for us, everyone was in the same state, it was pointless being anything but drunk throughout this experience. After six hours of rounds and tequilas, the first bus came to take us to the party. I needed to get on this bus else I was going to be on the bar floor. This moon party wasn't on the beach, it was in the forest which suited me because I hated the thought of getting sand in my shoes and my ass-crack. As drunk a man you will never see as me at that party, there was some horrendous dad dancing and a little tactical puke behind a tree, some nice breakfast for the birds in the morning.

Wednesday 5th April 2017

Nothing to report here other than the fact I wet the bed in the hostel and had the hangover from hell. I was genuinely gutted to have wet the bed, I hadn't done it since travelling. I informed Chevs who had no sympathy and just laughed at me. The worst part was that I didn't have the heart to tell the hostel that I had done this and I had to stay there that night. I couldn't sleep on my bottom bunk, you could've drowned a toddler on it, so I slept on a sofa that evening and we left promptly the morning after.

Thursday 6th April 2017

It was time to get our houses in order, we had a flight to catch in two days that would take us across to Melbourne, Australia for the next stage of our travels. We had to make our way to Singapore via boats and buses and we needed not to miss this flight so we pulled our sensible heads out from the very bottom of our rucksacks and glued them on temporarily. Us leaving it late meant that we spent a lot of time over the next couple of days on buses to get to Singapore Airport. In an ideal world, we would've spent a couple of nights in Singapore, but we had decided against this a few weeks back when looking at hostel prices there, they were too expensive for us.

Sunday 9th April 2017

We arrived at Singapore Airport about five hours before our flight because we were now sensible. We went over to check our luggage in so we could settle into a bar and discuss memories like the seasoned travellers we were by then. We were both tired and ready for an uncomfortable upright sleep on the plane. I showed the lady my email with my flight ticket which resulted in her having a confused look on her miserable face. After a few taps on a keyboard, she informed me that the flight was, in fact, tomorrow night and not that night. Computer says no. I looked at Chevs who had planned this leg of the journey so well right until the very end where he ballsed it right up. After a few moments of silence, we decided that we would sleep rough in the airport for the night. This meant McDonald's for dinner, McDonald's for breakfast tomorrow and another one for good measure for lunch.

The night's sleep was, as expected in an airport, non-existent. The airport remained busy overnight and the tannoy system didn't shut up for any longer than five minutes. Led on the floor in Singapore airport with my rucksack as a pillow, that was how my last night in SouthEast Asia was spent. Annoyingly, Chevs slept like a baby, he always does.

Australia

Tuesday 11th April 2017

Fuckin' Straylia! After breaking the world record for the longest amount of time spent continuously in Singapore Airport I finally landed on Australian soil. We had read up about getting into Australia and it seemed that all we needed to get through the border was a passport, the correct visa and $3000 Aussie Dollars in the bank. Chevs had seen himself dip below that by a few hundred dollars due to alcohol consumption and tattoo purchases so I transferred him some money across just to be on the safe side. There was no need, we walked through the border and were officially adopted Australians for the foreseeable future.

I had arranged for Jacob Botterell to come and pick us up from the airport which he was more than happy to do. I had met him when he came across to England for a summer to visit his grandparents who live in Yeovil. Our cricket captain at the time, Dick, met Botters in The Armoury on a Friday night, they both mumbled their way through a conversation about cricket and the next day he turned up still pretty drunk and played for us. The rest is history, Botters has gone down in Yeovil folklore because of his ability to sink pints, the fact he had two kebabs after a night out and, my favourite reason, he had shit himself in Wetherspoons, ran to the Esso garage to buy a can of deodorant, sprayed himself, threw the boxers away and made his way back into town to continue his night.

He arrived, beeped up and called me a cunt within the first few seconds. 'Welcome to the promised land!' He beamed. He lived a few miles outside of Melbourne but was going to drive us into the CBD (centre) and show us around before taking us down to our hostel in St Kilda. The first port of call was to get ourselves some decent food as all I had eaten over the last couple of days was three large McDonalds meals. If there was one thing I was certain of it was that Botters would know a good pub in Melbourne. We arrived and it was not too different from a pub in England. The big difference here and across the whole of Australia is that they serve schooners not pints. A schooner is about three-quarters of a pint and they apparently serve these because a pint would get too warm in the heat. My theory is that Australians are lightweights and can't handle pints, as proven by Botters shitting his pants in Spoons. Integrated into the pubs are betting terminals, so if you wanted to put a quick accumulator on or put a fiver on a horse you could do so in the comfort of the boozer under the influence of alcohol, dangerous.

We settled in for a chicken and chips with a schooner of 150 Lashes, what a beautiful drink that is by the way! At that moment in time, we had no set plans so there was a possibility that we would be staying in Melbourne, if the work was there this would've been both mine and Chevs's preferred destination. It would also mean seeing Botters more and potentially playing cricket with him again which was a lovely thought!

First things first, we needed to check in to our hostel and see what Melbourne had to offer. We had lots of bits to do over the next couple of days, mainly hunt for jobs and set up bank accounts. This is where sensible Chevs would come into his own and sort us both out with what we needed and I would follow him around like a man-child. Botters drove us down to the hostel and we checked in to Nomads. The only advice Botters gave us for our stay in Australia was 'Go to Gilligans in Cairns, it's madness!' Mental note taken.

Monday 17th April 2017

The phone call came from Chevs mate James who worked on a farm in Queensland. At the drop of a hat, I packed my life back into my rucksack again and bought a one-way ticket to Cairns, home of lots of farms and the infamous Gilligans. At this stage, I was trusting someone that Chevs had met a few times in a Southampton pub and I was a bit apprehensive about it if I am honest. But Chevs trusted him and that was enough for me, he had been a good judge of character up until now, other than the ladyboy that he fancied in Thailand. It was a strange feeling to be leaving for work so soon. All of a sudden it didn't feel like travelling anymore. It felt like living, I would be working, paying rent, doing food shops and all the other things that normal people of the world do. I wasn't mentally ready, I was still in travel mode.

Tuesday 18th April 2017

The flight up North was early and considering we would land in the same country it was three hours and twenty minutes long! Australia is massive!

As soon as we arrived in Cairns we checked into the hostel and both had emails asking us to travel up on the 21st to check in to Tolga Lodge. Tolga is a small place in the Atherton Tablelands known for its large farms full of mainly avocados and bananas, the lodge would place us on one of these farms and we would pay them rent for the privilege. I wasn't going to be fussy, I wanted to do farm work about as much as I wanted to boil to death so the sooner it was over and done with the better.

Tolga, Australia

Friday 21st April 2017

The start of my new life as a farmer. Back in Somerset, I had worked on farms previously picking wheat and barley in the summer whilst I was at university. I had hated it and that was relatively easy, this was set to be a lot more challenging. I jumped on the bus tentatively, thinking about what this next chapter would hold, I had no idea what was going to happen when we arrived in Tolga.

What happened was I got greeted by an extremely drunk Scottish man named Dean, it was no later than 8 pm and he was absolutely out of his tree. As we were handed the contract by Trish, the lodge owner, he told me 'Nae to fuckin' bother with it!' I had arrived at some form of happy farm, it wasn't just Dean that was drunk, almost everyone was, I suppose it was a Friday night. All I could hear was *'here we fucking go'* being shouted by more Scottish blokes outside, Tolga wasn't going to be a quiet one then. We signed our lives away and went to put our bags in our new home, a small room with two bunk beds sleeping four stinky blokes. The bottom bunks were already occupied by Sam and Dan, our two new roommates. Top bunks were the only option for newbies because they sucked ass and everyone who was already there didn't want to sleep in them. Sam and Dan, both English, wasted no time in getting us out of the room and out for a few beers with everyone, the perfect way to make introductions.

Tolga Lodge was like a rehab centre for travellers, everyone was itching to get their farm work done and then bugger off travelling again. That night I met the entirety of the Scottish lads who were with Dean, they were Gavin, Andy and Elliot. I didn't understand a whole lot of what was coming out of their mouths, but they told me to call Dean 'Spazzy Dean' so I did. It was clear to see how he had got that nickname. He would make a funny face and poke his tongue out when called it. Four dafties. My initial thoughts were that this was a good place to be, everyone was in the same shitty boat and were trying to make the most of it.

Sunday 23rd April 2017

The second piss-up in two days and this time I started early in a bid to try and get to the same sort of level as everyone else was on Friday. I had made friends with the Scots who knew my name now, so they were no longer just shouting '*new boy!*' at me. Sam and Dan from my room were also confirmed as good blokes. Sam had also introduced me to Jamie and Ted, two lads that he was travelling with and they both seemed alright as well. Throughout the all-day drinking session it became clear that I was going to enjoy my time here, it reminded me of university halls, everyone was very sociable and drunk mumbling was the mother tongue of everyone. It also became clear that I was probably going to be doing a fair few farm shifts hungover. Me becoming a functioning alcoholic during my time in Tolga was slashed to 1/3 on day two. That day I also met four Germans, Phil, Patricia, Dom and Christina. Phil was a long-serving member of Tolga Lodge and had been there for far too long already.

The lodge itself had a decent outside drinking area and a ping-pong table which was transformed into a beer pong table most of the time. I wasn't bad at beer-pong, but people had been getting a lot of practice in at the lodge, I didn't win a game all night. The positive of me being one of the worst at beer-pong was that I drank a lot of beer quite quickly, I was soon at 'Spazzy Dean' level. So was he.

Thursday 27th April 2017

Thursday night in Tolga meant that everyone went to the local pub, The Tolga Hotel, and drank $10 jugs until they couldn't stand. They weren't very inventive with names in Tolga, everything was "Tolga something' or 'The something Tolga.' It was nice to see everyone in a pub environment and not just sat outside of the lodge drinking tinnies like the local chavs. The $10 deal was a hit for the whole town as it was rammed with people. Farmers, oldies and backpackers alike came together for the once a week occasion of getting pissed a little bit cheaper than usual. Lovely.

Saturday 29th April 2017

Tried Goon (cheap boxed wine) for the first time and couldn't speak or see after half a box of it.

Monday 1st May 2017

I finally got the nod for some farm work and the good news was that I would be working with my best pal Benjamin Cheveralls. The bad news was that it was only a day's work helping a local old boy do some maintenance at the shooting range. A job is a job though and at that stage, I would've sold my body on the streets to get out of the lodge for a day.

The work itself was easy, all I had to do was jet wash the outside of a building and then do a little bit of painting. The old boy we were working with was nice, he had made up a packed lunch for us which was a very kind gesture. When I pulled the sandwich out and it filled was Tuna I nearly strangled him to death with the hosepipe. Chevs had two Tuna sandwiches for lunch, what a day he was having.

He took us to the cashpoint afterwards and paid us in cash for our 'hard' work, he was very appreciative and gave us $10 on top to get a pint that evening, what a gentleman. $80 for a day's work wasn't too bad at all, it would pay for my weekly food shop anyway which happened that night at the local Woolworths. Pasta, bread, pasta sauce, beers, it was like being a student again.

Wednesday 3rd May 2017

Another stint of farm work was organised, this time for a massive two whole days. At this rate, I was going to see my 30th Birthday celebrated in Tolga. My second job was working on a cabbage farm and it was again with Chevs, which was the only positive. Cabbage picking was as close to slave labour as I will ever get, who knew how heavy a bloody cabbage is! Some young Aussie bloke with three teeth and long hair would cut the cabbage out, chuck it to Chevs who would chuck it to me and I would chuck it in the back of the truck to be packed away safely. There was a whole day of this, catching cabbages, twisting and chucking them onto a truck a few metres away, I had enough of it within the first 15 minutes.

I managed a whole day and was bordering on exhaustion, muscles in my body ached that had never ached before, my hip joints had completely eroded and my legs just flopped around below me. I am now guaranteed to need a hip replacement later in life all because I chucked a few thousand cabbages around in a day. The thought of going back the next day made me more emotional than a drunk mum watching One Born Every Minute, but I knew I had to do it else I was never going to get put on a farm full time. I tried to think of the positives, maybe I would lose a bit of weight? Maybe I would go a nice bronze colour? I've never appreciated a dribbling cold shower and a top bunk as much as I did after that first day of cabbage picking.

Thursday 4th May 2017

I woke up stiffer than a virgin in a strip club, I could barely move my upper body. Day two of picking cabbages was going to be extremely difficult, I debated not going but Chevs, being the good guy that he is, dragged us both out of bed. Day two was worse, cabbages that were 10 kilograms now felt like they were 50 kilograms, I was just waiting for a cabbage to get thrown at me and my body to give up and collapse underneath me as I caught it. I didn't collapse and made it through my first two days of farm work, if I got placed on a cabbage farm there was no way on earth I was completing three months. I was so shattered after these two days that I didn't even make it down the pub for jugs of beer, Gavin called me 'A wee fuckin' softy.' I am not cut out to be a farmer.

Sunday 7th May 2017

HWFG! That means here we fucking go! I had learnt it off the Scots who shouted it regularly at almost anything. Cooking a lasagne? Here we fucking go! Starting a game of FIFA? Here we fucking go! The reason we were all shouting it that morning was that it was the day of Tolga Races. The races happened every month or so and the entire community descended on the racecourse including all of us dopey backpackers. It was clearly an event that everyone got drunk at, I worked this out for myself when Jamie passed me a beer at 10 am as I was just settling into my cornflakes.

Chance (his real name) lent me a shirt because I didn't have one. Chance had some good clobber considering he was travelling, he was going to remain stylish no matter where he was in the world. It was nice to everyone looking slightly more like humans instead of smelly farmers, everyone brushed up pretty well. I had a clean shaved bald noggin and a pair of small circular sunglasses on my face. On reflection, I looked like a soft Charles Bronson which wasn't a good look.

We walked up to the races and I proceeded to lose on every race. The three days of painting and cabbage hurling funded the day of crap betting on donkeys. We all then stumbled back to the pub and then back to the lodge where I drank until I was full to the throat. I did finally win a game of beer pong though, against a nearly asleep Phil.

Monday 8th May

Being hungover on your first day of any job is not a great first impression, but that was the impression my new boss was going to get of me. I had been placed on Lankester Farm and was going to be picking avocados for the foreseeable future. I had woken up still drunk and grabbed German Phil out of his bed as he was going to be working on the same farm as me. I had last seen Phil through blurry eyes asleep on the bench outside at 3 am. We both needed work like a hole in the bollocks, the fact it was 7 am and it was 32 degrees outside made matters so much worse. I got on the bus and slumped into my seat dreading my first day on this farm, I was already debating how much I wanted to get a second-year visa, it didn't seem worth it.

I arrived at this massive farm with a busload of enthusiastic people who were ready to pick avocados fast and ass lick some Australian farmer for three months. Phil and I needed to go unnoticed because we were going to be completely useless for the day.

'What're they doing here?' Mr Lankester said to the bus driver who had brought us down from the lodge, talking as if we weren't there. It was immediately clear to me that this bloke was an arrogant prick, fair enough he was probably a multi-millionaire. 'Well they aren't due here til tomorrow, take 'em back!' Without even a glance in our direction, he walked back into his barn where the avocados were being packed. Despite him being an ass hole, he had delivered the best news possible, Phil grabbed my arm with excitement and asked me if this was real or if he was dreaming. I informed Phil that it was real life and there were two beanbags at the lodge with our names on them!

We got back to the lodge, I made myself a pint of orange juice and lemonade, grabbed a large packet of tortilla crisps and parked myself on a beanbag in front of the TV with Phil. About five minutes into an episode of Fresh Meat I was away with the fairies and catching up on the sleep I so desperately needed. I had got away with that one, tomorrow when we turned up at Lankester I was going to be in much better shape, as long as no one wanted a beer later that evening.

Tuesday 9th May 2017

A much better start because I was not drunk and Mr Lankester wanted us on his farm. My sober verdict on Mr Lankester was that he was indeed an arrogant prick. We wouldn't see much of him though as he was too busy counting his stacks of money in his humongous house. We were under the supervision of a team leader named Marty, a proper bogan Aussie. Pick fruit, drink piss, smoke weed and talk shit was hit motto. He handed us a ladder each and told us what to do. Please read the following in your best bogan Australian accent for authenticity. 'Place your ladder on flat ground so ya don't fuckin' fall, get yourself up to the top, pick the Avo's and then make your way down. Make sure ya bag is full before ya come over here n' chuck em in the trailer. Don't leave any in the fuckin' tree because I'll spot it and lose me shit.'

Cheers Marty, message received. Picking avocados was immediately easier than hurling cabbages about. It was still difficult, and my bag of avocados would get pretty heavy once it was full. The bag was strapped around my back and shoulders so the pouch for the avocados was at the front, just like putting a rucksack on backwards. After the first day of picking, there was some slight pain in my back, but nothing compared to last week's pain. Marty would pick two avocados for everyone else's one, I have never seen anyone climb a ladder and pick fruit so quickly with a cigarette in their mouth, he was a master of his art.

Thursday 11th May 2017

This was the first Thursday that I felt I had earned the right to get drunk on $10 jugs. Three full days of picking avocados had taken it out of me and I needed a beer, it felt like if I didn't have a jug of beer I was going to pass away. Everyone was in the same headspace, so we all changed from smelly farm clothes to still quite smelly casual clothes and got down the pub. I caught up with Chevs over a jug and he was also finding his farm to be bearable, it felt strange to be having a drink with him after work again. The last time we had done that he was pulling me a pint in Southampton and I was wearing a sky-blue tunic.

Friday 12th May 2017

With every thirty Thursday comes a bad Friday only this one was even worse because I had to go to work picking fruit. The only silver lining of this extremely dark cloud was that we would finish at lunchtime, a little perk of working at Lankester Farm. This day goes down as one of the worst in my whole life, I was dehydrated, dizzy and sweating pure 150 Lashes. I vowed to never work another farm shift hungover but when I said it out loud Phil laughed at me and I realised what I had said. This was going to be the first of many!

To confirm that my head was on its way off I decided to dye the little hair that I had on my head blonde when I returned to the lodge making me look like a receding Slim Shady, a truly awful look for me.

Phil was also in the mood for blonde hair so followed suit and also did his eyebrows.

Monday 15th May 2017

Jack, a new English lad at the lodge, joined us on Lankester farm. He was a bit northern and dangerously laid back, he was in neutral and wasn't coming out of it for anyone. To pass the time I had asked Phil if he would teach me some basic German because picking avocados in silence was starting to drive me round the bend. I wondered if anyone had considered using farm work as a form of torture or maybe as punishment for minor criminals like thieves and drug dealers. Phil taught me as much German as he could, but my brain just isn't made for learning a new language. I can remember trying to learn French at school and it just being impossible to get my head around. I learnt bonjour on day one and thought it was easy but proceeded to learn very little else, nothing helpful anyway, when is counting to 20 in French badly ever going to help me? German was the same, Phil drilled me but all I learnt and can still remember to this day is Goodun Morgan V Gets Der – Good Morning, how're you? That and Smetaling – butterfly. Phil wasn't the best German teacher mind you, he would laugh at my poor efforts and then try and teach me swear words in the place of normal words. If I ever walk into a German bar and ask for a 'small twat' it is on Phil.

Thursday 18th May 2017

By this stage Scottish Andy would say to me every morning at breakfast 'Harry my boy, getting on it tonight?' Which would be followed by a 'Yeeehaw' from Elliot. Everyone knew the answer to that question, it was a yes from me. I introduced everyone at the farm to Vince, my extremely drunk alter-ego. Phil and I didn't bother with any dinner that night and just got straight on the goon for an entrée. Our main course was jugs at the pub and we did not make the desert. This was the first time in Australia that I had fully pulled the pin and I went off spectacularly. Tolga is the only place I have ever been where everyone got just as silly as me, there wasn't a sober human insight.

I woke up on Friday morning and had wet the top bunk, it was absolutely soaked. I felt like I had probably been about five times in the night. Making matters worse was the fact I was still fully clothed and had my phone in my pocket which was now completely soaked in my urine and not working. This was a real low point for me. I can't explain the feeling of waking up drenched in urine and knowing that you can't just lie in bed hungover, it sucks real bad. I also had to inform Sam and Dan that I had pissed in their home which is not what anyone wants to hear. That was my first sicky of my time in Tolga, I hate calling in sick but I was covered in wee and not able to see straight so I had no other option, Phil was also still in bed and did not make it to the farm. I put my phone in rice as advised by Google, but it was long gone, dead to the world. What a way to go, drowned in piss. I hadn't backed anything up on the cloud either so all of my photos of my dogs and travels disappeared. I wasn't angry, I was disappointed in myself.

Saturday 20th May 2017

The wheels were coming off and there was nothing I could do to stop them. Everyone around me wanted to get drunk and I didn't have a no button. If it wasn't Gavin wanting a beer it was Ted if it wasn't Ted it was Chevs and this was a never-ending cycle. The owners had noticed that we were all getting drunk a lot and Pompy, Trish's husband and co-owner, came up for a chat. He chose the wrong time as it was 4 pm and a lot of us had been drinking since midday. The Scots took none of Pompy's pep talk on, it was greeted with a 'Get tae fuck!' He informed us that the neighbours had complained a couple of times now so we needed to keep it down else they would have to enforce a curfew. No one wanted a curfew, but we couldn't help ourselves, we were all too far gone. We needed straitjackets, not a pep talk. Instead of that day getting quieter it got livelier and 100% of the occupants of the lodge joined in for drinks. This night was the pinnacle of Tolga Lodge, everyone was carefree and enjoying themselves like they should on a Saturday when they picked fruit all week for shit money.

Sunday 21st May 2017

Curfew enforced, Goon was banned as was music after 10 am. Uproar in the lodge and a very sad day indeed. The only thing that made Tolga Lodge bearable was the social side of it after work and at the weekend, that would be no longer, I didn't want to talk to anyone sober, how boring.

Tuesday 23rd May 2017

Looking back, this was when I had completely lost the plot. A mixture of picking avocados, sleeping on a top bunk and drinking goon had got to me and I was on the road to self-destruction. Marty had talked shit on the farm all day about how he could fight a wild dog and how he was the best shooter in Queensland. The morale on the farm was at an all-time low, everyone was fed up picking these stupid green things from a tree and chucking them in a trailer to make Mr Lankester another $10,000. As we got back on the bus that took us back to the lodge a chap from the other hostel in Tolga punched laid back Jack in the head for no apparent reason, it was all going wrong! The final straw for me was someone eating my meat feast pizza that I had wanted that night, it tipped me over the edge and I pressed the detonate button located in my brain.

Jamie was fed up as well so we wrongly decided to get a box of goon in and get as drunk as we possibly could. It was only Jamie, Phil and I properly drinking, a few joined throughout the night, but it was us three slightly depressed lads drinking boxes of cheap wine.

Thursday 25th May 2017

Well, it was a Thursday, you can fill in the gaps.

Friday 26th May 2017

The day had come. Trish had finally had enough of me and told me with her best Barbara Windsor impression 'Get out my Lodge.' It was completely understandable, I had been on a month bender at the lodge, it had turned out to be a party hostel. I was slightly annoyed because there were probably another 20 people she could've booted out of the lodge but she singled me out, I don't think she ever really liked me. Phil had been on the beers with me every single time yet didn't even get a talking to, the untouchable German. I'm guessing they were scared of the Scots because if Pompy had come to tell them to leave I'm pretty sure Andy would've punched his head off. So, it was me who got his marching orders after just over a month of living in Tolga Prison for underpaid farmworkers.

It was a bittersweet feeling for me, I would be leaving a job that I hated and a lodge that was no good at all, but I would also be leaving a lot of new friends that had become a weird little family. Of course, the real sickener was that I was going to be leaving Chevs, a man who I had spent the last four months travelling with and whom without I was incredibly useless. I can remember his face vividly as I told him I was getting kicked out of the lodge. He smiled and laughed because he knew that it was typical of me, but he then realised that this meant I would be leaving town. 'Where will you go?' He asked. At that point, I had absolutely no idea.

Saturday 27th May 2017

I couldn't leave Tolga immediately because I had nowhere to go so I decided to stay local for a week or so whilst I sorted out a plan. I moved into The Tolga Hotel located directly above the local pub. I had spoken to the landlord and his bar staff on many occasions and got on with them pretty well. It was also considerably cheaper to live above the pub and I had my room with good WiFi and some lovely hot showers. Tolga Lodge was ripping me and everyone else who stayed there off. The best option for me was to go to Perth as I had a friend there who I could stay with whilst I looked for work. I got in touch with Ash on Facebook and he was more than happy to have me. Ash and I had played cricket in Yeovil before he moved away with his girlfriend who is Australian to start his little family. I was looking forward to seeing him and was praying that I was able to find work there.

Tuesday 30th May 2017

Jack had enough of the lodge as well and came to stay in the hotel with me. Our views were the same on the place, hugely overpriced accommodation, greedy owners and shite work. He had no plans, so I asked Ash if he had room for one more at his place in Perth which he did. So just like that, I had a travelling partner again for an escape to the West Coast of Australia.

Saturday 3rd June 2017

Someone in the Lodge had heard that Mareeba was quite a good night out and that was all the persuasion we needed. It was a 45-minute drive North of Tolga and Dom agreed to drive one of the buses and took 15 of us there for a tear up. I snuck into the lodge for a quick pre-drink and to say hello to everyone who I had strangely missed over the last week. When Trish gave me the boot she meant it, my name was not to be spoken, I was like a fat, blonde Voldemort.

Mareeba was by no stretch of the imagination a lively place, but it was certainly busier than sleepy Tolga. There were a couple of decent bars in the town centre which we spent our night in. I bought a bottle of champagne as a leaving and 'sorry for being such a pillock' present. This was a great idea until I was kicked out of the bar for having the bottle of champagne on the dance floor. Me singing 'It's champagne on the dancefloor' to the tune of murder on the dance floor by Sophie Ellis-Bexter did not help the bouncers mood.

Jamie and I wandered into the bar across the road which was a lot quieter but had a little disco room floor and was playing some bangers. There was a fancy-dress party in there and I tried very hard to seduce Wonder Woman who politely declined. Without question, the best part of the night was the McDonalds at the end of it. I had never wanted a chicken mayo so much so I ordered five and ate them all before Dom left the car park.

Sunday 4th June 2017

My leaving date couldn't have fallen on a better day, it was the Tolga Races again and everyone was in the mood to get wild. Spazzy Dean was wearing white shorts, an open white shirt and sunglasses looking like something off of Love Island. He needed to wear the glasses because his eyes were glazed over as he was an absolute right off by 1 am. This was a much more successful day at the races, mainly because everyone from the lodge attended because the weather was nicer than the previous meet. It was so good to see everyone and say goodbye properly and apologise to anyone who I may have pissed off, mainly Chevs, Dan and Sam. I also won some money on a couple of horses so came out of the races $200 up, although once I spent the following few hours inside the pub the profit was not looking so healthy.

This was not a farewell to Tolga, it was good riddance. If it wasn't for the incredible people that I had met at the lodge I think I would've left within a couple of days. A special mention must go to Gavin, Andy, Elliott and Dean who I genuinely think are the funniest and nicest guys I have ever met, I will visit Scotland and get silly with them one day and I am sure it will get out of hand. Also, to Phil who was wired up wrong just like me! On a serious note, something needs to change regarding the farm work in Australia, they do take the piss. You work long hours doing hard, manual labour and half of your paycheck goes on the rent and bills. As for Tolga Lodge itself, the best thing that could happen to that place is it goes into administration and closes down forever. As Andy used to chant, "Fuck you Pompy you'll never win the league!' It didn't make sense then and it doesn't now but it does seem fitting.

Perth, Australia

Wednesday 7th – Wednesday 21st June 2017

I landed in Perth with an awful blonde hair cut and liver failure pending, Tolga had chewed me up and spat me back out. I was thankful to have Franko in Perth who had a bed and might be able to help me find work. Jack ideally wanted to save some more money before heading home too so jobs were top of the to-do list. We jumped in a taxi on arrival and headed for Ash's place which was located in Wanneroo just north of the city. It was a quiet suburb of Perth and there were a few fruit farms around so we were going to try our luck getting some work there even if it meant picking avocados again. What farmer wouldn't want someone with 1 month's previous experience in picking avocados on their farm? Franko's place was just what I needed after months of average hostels, he had a comfortable sofa, a massive TV and I had a room all to myself.

Finding a job in Perth proved more difficult than finding the final few Horcruxes in Harry Potter, there was nothing about. Jack and I searched the job boards high and low but unless you were a skilled man you were going to struggle. I am not a skilled man and neither was Jack so we were up shit creek without a boat. Strangely there were no jobs advertised for an in-experienced journalist with a Desmond 2:2. The only way we had a chance of getting a job here was by getting into the city centre and physically asking shops and businesses if they were recruiting. Franko had a Peugeot convertible designed strictly for hairdressers and was happy to let us drive it into the city to see if we could work some magic and find a job. All the will in the world wasn't going to get me a job in Perth, not a single place was hiring, it was a soul-destroying effort just getting frequent 'nopes' from loads of Aussies.

It was a real shame this didn't work out because the best option for me was staying with Franko and working in Perth, that would have been the perfect outcome for me over the next few months. But that wasn't to be so I needed a plan B and that's where Jack came in. He had worked in a remote part of Australia in some sort of hotel

110

for the first six months of his time in Australia. He said these places were great because you lived on the site, food was sometimes included and the work was just regular bar and restaurant work. I had never done this sort of work before but thought I'd give it a good go, I had nothing else on the agenda. I signed up to the website and waited for the phone calls and emails to flood in when hotel owners realised they could have an English chap with no experience but a degree in Sports Journalism from the 127th best university in the UK working for them. They didn't come. Three days passed and I hadn't even had a scam phone call come through to the cheap phone that I had purchased at Woolworths following 'wet the top bunk gate' in Tolga. How unemployable was I? Had Tolga Lodge sent out a communication to all backpacker employers and warned them about me?

Finally, an email from the recruitment agency. A chap called Jamie wanted to give me a telephone interview regarding a potential job in Weipa working at The Albatross Bay Resort. A quick Google showed me that this place was as far north as you could go in Australia before falling off the edge of the country, it's so North the territory it is located in is called Far North Queensland. If this was a job in the UK it would've been located in John O'Groats. Beggars can't have a choice, choosers. Jamie called later that evening and we chatted for a good hour about Weipa, the job, himself and me. He was a Kiwi and over the phone sounded like a great bloke, he liked sport, beer and just wanted a member of staff to be able to pull a schooner and help out here and there. I may have lied to him about being able to pull a schooner, but it was just a little white one. He said, 'you've pulled a schooner before?!' And I harmlessly agreed. 'Have I? Haha, why would I apply for a job at a resort without ever pouring a schooner before? Of course, I have!' I hadn't. Not a single schooner or pint in my life but it wasn't going to be the hardest thing to learn was it? It wasn't like I was lying about holding a pilot's license before ending up in the front seat of a Boeing 747.

White lie executed perfectly, Jamie offered me the job there and then bearing in mind we had never seen each other before and had only spoken for an hour. I'll be honest, at the time I wasn't sure if this was going to be a sensible move for me, but it was the best option I had. Weipa, Far North Queensland, Ass End of Nowhere, Australia. That was going to be my next home on this crazy adventure.

I bought the flights and celebrated with Franko that weekend by going into Perth for muchos beeros. Jack was only a week behind me, he landed himself another job in a remote location too. I am forever grateful to Ash for taking me in for a couple of weeks at a time where I didn't know my ass from my elbow. I had levelled out and was no longer the clinically insane person that screamed '*avocado!*' in his sleep after chugging goon. I was ready for a sensible chapter in which I would save a bit of money and people would remark about what a professional young man I was.

Weipa, Australia

Friday 23rd June 2017

It was a real mission getting to Weipa. I had to fly from Perth to Townsville, Townsville to Cairns and then Cairns to Weipa. There aren't many flights in and out of Weipa due to it being a very remote location. The only people that flew there were those working on the mines or travelling to the tip of Australia and of course me. I've always found the fact that the top of Australia was named the tip funny because in England the tip is where you go and throw all of your rubbish. I felt that it was safe for me to assume that I wasn't about to fly into a large landfill at the top of Australia.

Weipa Airport was and still is the smallest airport I have ever flown into. It was a dusty runway with a large shed and one security guard stopping any mischief happening. It took all of five minutes to exit the plane and walk through security to collect my bag. I was greeted by Sandy who was the Restaurant Manager at The Albatross Bay Resort, she was going to be my tour guide and help me settle in. Imagine Dawn French but Australian and not quite as funny, that's Sandy. We drove for 30 minutes talking about the resort, what she did and what I'd be doing before reaching the little town of Weipa. We drove past Woolworths which she pointed out and told me there was also a hairdresser in there should I ever need it. My hair was still very bad and blonde so I joked with Sandy that there was no sorting my barnet out! In Weipa, the mullet was an acceptable and popular haircut so I wouldn't have the worst hair there amazingly. Up the road was the Golf Club and the Bowls Club and that was it, my new home. Tour of Weipa over, we turned into the Albatross which was immediately a lot bigger than I imagined. It was made up of a Drive-Thru alcohol shop, a sports bar, a restaurant and about 150 rooms. I imagined a bar and 30 rooms maximum.

Sandy took me into reception where I met Baylee and Jane. Baylee was the Assistant Manager and was immediately lovely. Jane was the Reception Manager and was immediately a miserable cow. Thankfully Baylee was the one who showed me around the resort and introduced me to those who I would be working and living with for the next however many months. I walked into the kitchen and met Richie the head chef, Joey and Tony. We walked through the kitchen and into the bar and met Asta, Jacqui and Dean. Dean and Asta were both bar managers of some sort, Jacqui was just really attractive. We then walked down to the Drive-Thru which was a bottle shop in which you could just drive through it and buy alcohol, like a McDonalds for booze. At the Drive-Thru, I met Mason who was worried about the square root of fuck all. Then we walked across to where I would be living. The staff quarters were at the back of the resort and had one side for the blokes and another for the ladies. On the left-hand side and three doors deep on a veranda was my door. Baylee informed me that my new next-door neighbours were Nathan and Nigel. Very helpful was Baylee, she left me and I was in my room alone, for the first time since moving into university halls I was nervous. I didn't know anyone here, only Baylee very briefly and Jamie from a phone call. I was genuinely scared of how this was going to all pan out. What if everyone hated me? What if I wasn't as funny in Weipa? Well, I would find out shortly but first things first I needed to get my head down in my new room which had a double bed and air conditioning. Talk dirty to me.

Monday 26th June 2017

I had met a few people over the previous couple of days and no one had told me they hated me yet so I was slightly less nervous. I had my first shift in the Drive-Thru starting at 9 am and would be shadowing Mason who would teach me everything I needed to know. Mason was an incredibly decent bloke and if he was any more laid back he would've fallen over. I arrived at 9 sharp and watched and listened to Mason go about his work. It certainly wasn't a stressful job that is for sure. Throughout the morning there were about 20 customers and a lot of the time was spent sitting on our thumbs. The only very important thing to do was to ask everyone for ID as there were certain areas of the Far North where alcohol is illegal. People weren't allowed to purchase alcohol if they had one of the restricted areas on their driving licence, simple. This didn't mean they wouldn't try their luck, the first customer of the day was someone that Mason knew and before he even took his ID out Mason said 'you know you can't take alcohol home bro!' To which he replied 'na I'm taking it to my mums down the road.' They would try anything to get hold of some alcohol. Their favourite thing to drink was wine and Divas which was a wine-based spirit that was said to blow your head off, like goon mixed with vodka.

It remained quiet throughout the day and I picked up everything that I needed to know. First shift completed. I had also made good enough friends with Mason that I could nod and say hello next time I saw him.

Thursday 29th June 2017

As well as the Drive-Thru bottle shop, the Albi also owned a store in the local shopping centre, the same one Sandy had driven me past that consisted of Woolworths, a hairdresser, a charity shop, a department store and the bottle shop. The store was much smaller and was stocked wall to wall with booze. Eloise was my babysitter for the day and showed me the ropes in the store, the same rules applied in terms of identification. I soon found that people would try both bottle shops on the same day which was why there was regular contact with the Drive-Thru to let them know who had been about and vice versa. It was nice to watch people walk into the shop thinking they had a chance to buy some alcohol and see Eloise shut them down immediately. 'Derek, you've already been to the Drive-Thru this morning, Mason has called me, what makes you think you're gonna get served here?' And like a toddler that has just received a good telling off, they would leave.

Alcohol in Weipa was extremely expensive compared to anywhere else I had been in Australia and even the world. A crate of 24 bottles of 150 Lashes was $75 (£45), even the cheaper Great Northern Beers you were looking at £30 for a crate. It was enough to make me debate not drinking during my time in Weipa, a debate that lasted about three seconds in my brain before deciding I would need a beer or eight at some stage.

Saturday 1st July 2017

Weipa was constantly hotter than the Sun. There was no break in the heat in this place, it was constantly cooking at around 35 degrees and on a hot day, it would break 40. There was no breeze to speak of either, just 100% humidity to make me even more uncomfortable. I left the air conditioning on in my room constantly and it eventually became like a fresh winter morning in Somerset in there which was delightful. I'd go from sweating in shorts and a vest to shivering in a jumper within minutes.

After my Drive-Thru shift, I headed for a few beers with Eloise and Nathan at the Bowls Club, I hadn't met Nathan properly yet despite him being my neighbour. I had met my other neighbour, Nige, who was one of the chefs. He was peculiar but harmless, he kept himself to himself, listened to death metal and smoked about 60 fags a day. Remember when Ian Beale ended up being a tramp in Eastenders? Give him Australian accent and you've got yourself Nige.

Nathan and I walked over to Eloise's room and made the short walk across to the Bowlies and I was pleasantly surprised with how nice the place was. In England, the Bowls Clubs are mainly for those who aren't far off the cemetery. Weipa's Bowls Club was a big bar with a nice outside seating area and loads of slot machines that the Aussies called 'The Pokies.' Eloise explained that there was a problem with addiction in Weipa, some people could play on the machines for a whole day only moving for a beer and a toilet break. I have only ever put £2 in a fruit machine in England and lost it immediately, so these slot machines didn't have any appeal to me despite the flashing lights and huge jackpots!

It was nice to meet Nate properly, he was a man-mountain from New Zealand and wouldn't have looked out of place pulling trucks on the TV. He was also gay, but not the skip up to you and say heyyyy kind. I wouldn't have ever guessed, he was slightly camp but no more than I am, although he did drink Bacardi and coke which should've been a tell.

Monday 3rd July 2017

I wasn't aware at the time, but this day changed my time in Weipa for the better. Matthew Cureton arrived at the Albi and doubled the number of English people within a 1000-mile radius. I can remember clear as day this tall, ginger chap walking down to put his stuff in his room as I sat out on the veranda. Jamie had told me that another English chap would be joining the team which was very exciting. 'Alright lad, ow's it going?' He shouted across to me in his Northern accent. I walked over to his room which was behind mine and we made our introductions. We loved football and boozing and with that, I had just made my best mate in Weipa. 'Cor this room is alright innit, double bed, a bit of me that!' He was wandering around his room like Deon Dublin on Homes Under the Hammer. There was absolutely no doubt in my mind that we were going to get on like a house on fire for however long we were in this Northern fireball of a town. I also knew that it was going to lead in too many beers during my stay, sensible me wasn't going to last long.

Thursday 6th July 2017

The hardest shift at the Albi was the restocking of the bottle shop. All the alcohol was delivered to the resort and some of it needed transporting to the shop which meant making up pallets of beers, wines and spirits, driving them to the bottle shop and then unloading them all. It was like a HITT workout that lasted two hours in 34-degree heat. The only bonus of this shift was that I was doing it with Matt who was a big rugby player so made the reasonably heavy crates of beer look like pillows. I tried my best to keep up but the fact I hadn't worked out since college meant I was as weak as an Apple Sours shot. It was a pretty tedious task and one that involved lots of searching for different bottles of wine and obscure spirits and was the first manual labour I had done since picking avocados in Tolga. Whenever I felt like my back was hurting I thought back to the two days of cabbage picking and suddenly my back would feel better. I still do that to this day.

Other than dropping and smashing a bottle of wine it was a successful shift. I thought I was going to get a good bollocking for dropping the wine but Jamie just told me to write it down, it was only a cheap bottle. A cheap bottle being £9, some bottles were £30 plus, I didn't want to be dropping too many of them. Like Del Boy and Rodney Matt and I drove this truck full of booze down to the bottle shop and unloaded it for Eloise to pack away. We were one crate of Victoria Bitter down, not bad on our first ever attempt at it! My hands and biceps were sore and I was pretty sure I had heatstroke. I had to work the late shift of the Drive-Thru with Mason that evening which I could've done without.

Working the late shift meant doing a stock count which was about as fun as a poke in the eye with a hot stick. This was the one thing that Jamie was strict on, it was vital for him to know how much alcohol we had at both locations. In the past, people had just taken bottles of rum for themselves and called it a miscount. He told me a story about how one chap had just sat in the cooler drinking beer on his shift and wrote it down as wastage. He got caught out when Jamie popped across to get some ice for his beer cooler and he was absolutely steaming in the fridge. He was sacked on the spot. I nearly told Jamie about when I had been sacked on the spot at ParcelForce but thankfully my brain intercepted the thought. Safe to say when Jamie came down and realised that I had seemingly counted the stock with my eyes closed he was pretty pissed off. He asked me if I was just guessing or if I was thick as shit. The answer was probably a both but I refrained from telling him. He then took me around and did the recount with me, I was only 1200 cans of Great Northern and 30 bottles of Morgan Spiced Rum out, in my defence I hadn't counted or used any times tables since I was 12.

Saturday 8th July 2017

After everyone had finished their different shifts those who were available went down to the beach located at the back of the Albi for a few beers and a bonfire. It was a nice beach, the only downside was the fact that there were alligators in the water that could pop out and eat me alive at any time. 'Never fuckin' seen one, they don't like the heat of the fire!' Tony was an experienced fisher and he said this confidentially enough for me to risk my life. I ensured that I was sitting in the middle of everyone so that if an alligator did turn up it would eat one of them first and give me a chance to run. I back myself to outrun an alligator anyway, the key is to zig-zag.

This allowed me to meet Thais, Eirene, Corina, Tony and Sean who I had only been able to say hello to very briefly as I hadn't worked any shifts with them. Thais was from Spain and was a lone traveller who was out to find herself, Eirene was from Malaysia and had the biggest smile I have ever seen on someone who was only four foot eleven. Corina was an Aussie and slightly away in her cuckoo world but in a nice way, she would certainly not say no to smoking some weed if it was available, a super chilled woman. Sean was quiet and was leaving soon anyway so there was no point in us becoming mates. He had a guitar around a campfire like a typical traveller twat. Tony was an experienced head and wasn't arsed about anything. A more laid-back person I will probably never meet. He made Mason seem uptight.

There were a lot of names for me to remember at this stage but at least I was making some friends. Slowly but surely Weipa was beginning to feel a bit more homely.

Monday 10th July 2017

My white lies to ensure I got the job also led me to tell Jamie over the phone that I had worked in a restaurant before which was not true. The closest I had got to working in a restaurant was serving up some dinner in one of the care homes I used to work in back in Yeovil. Whatever the opposite of a Michelin star is was the level of food I had served. The Albi's restaurant was quite a fancy place, those who were at the hotel had paid a fair amount of money for their stay so the food and restaurant itself was lovely. The majority of the seating was outside and overlooking the beach which was a great setting. Sandy, the lovely lady who had picked me up from the airport, was going to be showing me the ropes and it all started very badly. 'You've done this before, so I won't take up too much of your time.' Was her opening line.

'Ahhh. You see, the thing is Sandy it's completely different in the UK, you know? Different plate sizes, lots of forks.' I needed a lot of her time, I had never carried a plate from the kitchen to a table before in my life.

Jacqui, the really attractive one, was working the shift as well and was carrying all kinds of plates and glasses at the same time. Why would someone want me coming to their table with their food and not sexy Jacqui? Surely I could just leave her to do all the plate carrying, I'd just clear tables and chill.

'SERVICE' Richie shouted from the kitchen. The food looked very good so it would've been a real shame if I had dropped it on the floor. Here goes nothing. Confidence was key, I burst through the door like I knew what I was doing and saw two plates of food waiting for me, I had already bitten off more than I could chew. Sandy pulled the ticket down and told me the food was going to table 26. I knew where that was because I'd memorised the table plan like a good student. I psyched myself up and went straight in for the two plates, just grabbing the ends of them and going for it. About halfway into the walk to table 26, I could feel my fingers breaking under the pressure of the plates, this was not the way I was supposed to be carrying them. The thought of Richie throwing a knife into my head kept me going and I arrived at table 26 with a fake smile and slid the plates onto the table. I had only dropped a couple of chips on the way, success! I was supposed to ask, 'who's ordered the steak?' and then place it down but I didn't have the strength. I got lucky and slid the food in-front of its rightful owner. On the way back I picked the chips from the floor and ate them.

I had to pull Jacqui to one side and tell her my little secret. I told her that I didn't need to carry three plates like her, I just want to carry two comfortably. She put a plate into the palm of my hand and spread my fingers so the weight was distributed evenly, it was much easier than my grab and dash method. I was ready for more food to carry now and that was good because there was a busload of people arriving in the restaurant for their dinner. There were actually bus tours that came up through Weipa and to the tip so a busload of people is no exaggeration. Four hours flew by, I was back and forth from the kitchen constantly, sweating and aching. Jacqui was bounding around the place carrying loads of plates and serving pints all at the same time, where was her inner strength and coordination coming from because I needed some.

Wednesday 12th July 2017

Introducing Harry the barman. This was the most nervous I have ever been to start a job, I had never made an alcoholic beverage behind a bar in my life and was expected to be a good barman instantly. I had watched a couple of YouTube tutorials on how to pull a schooner and it looked simple enough, tilt the glass, pour the drink and then straighten the glass as it fills leaving a lovely little head. What could go wrong?

I walked into the bar and was greeted by Dean and Asta who were both watching a dog race on the TV. "Go...go... go you good thing!' Dean was talking to the TV, he loved his dog and horse racing. Dean showed me around the place, guiding me through the different beers on tap and what we had in bottles. He also showed me how to use the till which was relatively simple and I was quite confident that I was going to be alright at this. My first customer came to the bar and ordered himself a schooner of Great Northern and my brain began instructing me. I tilted the glass and began to pour the beer and it pissed out everywhere! It came out so much faster than I expected. The result was a beer that was 75% head and good to no one, a pathetic effort.

'Got a flake for that.' Dean shouted from across the bar, a fair comment because it looked more like a 99 than a beer. I said that I was used to pouring beer into pint glasses, proper drinks. It was an excuse that Dean saw right through, luckily the chap who was buying was very thirsty so he took a large sip and just asked me to top it up with some more.

Schooner number two was nothing short of perfection, the pour was slower and the head was perfect. Dean looked at me like a proud father and I was now an ok barman. Things got a bit confusing when people ordered food because I had to give them a buzzer and I kept forgetting. I also kept forgetting to take stuff off of orders so ended up walking down to the kitchen to inform them that there was no cheese required on the burger that had just come through. All in all, it was a pretty successful shift.

Friday 14th July 2017

Another day, another restaurant shift. I was less anxious about picking up plates this time around which was nice. It was a relatively calm shift other than meeting Nicole properly for the first time who was on the crazy spectrum. If you made me a blonde Australian female then I would be Nicole, we were the same person, it was so strange. We had the same stupid sense of humour and the same stories of being too drunk and making idiots of ourselves. We danced awfully and sang out of tune to the restaurant music all shift. It was only a matter of time before we would get our hands on some wine and make idiots of ourselves together.

Wednesday 19th July 2017

Sandy had left the Albi with her partner Pat and moved home I think, awfully I can't remember. Sandy was lovely but her partner, Pat, had a face like a bulldog that had just eaten a stinging nettle! The role as Restaurant Manager was filled by Vicki who Nicole had known from her time working on some fancy island resort in Australia. Nicole reliably informed me that Vicki was a fucking legend. If that was her opinion, I was certain I would get on with her too. I did, I worked in the restaurant that evening with Vicki, Nicole and Jacqui and my sides hurt with laughter. Vicki was somewhere between tough and glamorous, she'd call me darling and then moments later be arguing with the chefs about a food complaint. My finger also hurt as I had picked a steak knife up at the wrong end which had resulted in a little cut on my index finger. I overreacted and ensured that everyone knew how brave I was for completing the shift. Vicki had arrived to shake things up in the restaurant. All of a sudden fancy bottles of water and table decorations were dotted around, I had to wear a pair of shoes and not just my trainers, it was all getting a bit posh and rightly so although I struggled, I do not have that setting, I am more Shameless than Downton Abbey.

Friday 21st July 2017

It was finally time to plug in at the Albi and get drunk with everyone. By now I was on good terms with most of the staff and it seemed that everyone was comfortable enough to get a little bit twisted down the beach. It was good to see everyone together drinking and laughing, everyone had stories to tell and the drunker we got the better they got! The drinks went on well into the early hours when only Thais, Corina, Tony and I were left drinking and chatting. By this stage, I was calling out the local alligators telling them that I could outrun them.

Part of me was sure that Thais was flirting with me and the other half was remembering that I had the pulling skills of an armless man. She was laughing at my stories but then again everything was funny after two bottles of wine. I didn't think too much into it and continued drinking and telling Corina to not fall asleep on the beach. I told them the story of me running over a puppy on my birthday which they didn't enjoy, no one ever does. We all called it a night at 4 am, it was getting lighter and Tony had to work a breakfast shift in the kitchen the mad man!

Monday 24th July 2017

I was tasked with doing The Pokies for the shift. This meant wearing a buzzer and attending to the winners and those just wanting to change up their big notes into coins. The Pokies was busier than peak Times Square, New York. The buzzer went off almost constantly with people winning anything from $10 - $1000+ and with every buzz I lost a part of my soul. No one would cash out on a round number either, every payout was $117.84 or $34.17 which may not seem a huge problem, but I was fumbling and dropping coins all over the floor. Dean, Nicole and Asta kept me sane throughout this shift which by the end of it I wanted to throw the buzzer and myself into the sea. I clocked out and walked to the reception area to get some WiFi to FaceTime home and finally admitted to them that I had been kicked out of the lodge in Weipa and didn't just leave off my own back. I could see their disappointment through my pixilated iPad screen.

Friday 28th July 2017

There was another arrival at the Albi and his name was Dean just to confuse matters. Dean Furber had joined us and was going to be the Bar/Drive-Thru manager. To ensure we never got confused, Matt and I decided to call Dean Hayman Deano and Dean Furber just Dean, they looked nothing alike. Dean got lucky and his first-ever shift in the Drive-Thru was with me on a Friday night, the busiest night of the week. I had no problems now, I was elite at asking for ID and refusing alcohol. I was also not bad at counting which for a 23-year-old man was expected, I was only out by the odd few on my counts now unlike the 1200 on my first shift. Dean and I took a good fisting that night, it was non-stop from start to finish. We closed the shutters at 9 pm and then had to completely restock the place which took us both another hour, it was a tough first shift for Dean. I reassured him that it wasn't normally like this as I didn't want him to be on the next plane out of there, he seemed like a good bloke.

Tuesday 1st August 2017

Things had started to liven up at the Albi now that everyone knew each other. Matt and I had decided that it would be good to get everyone together for a night in the Common Room for lots of beers and drinking games, a little bit of team bonding. Most of those available came to the drinking session and it was good to see everyone out of their work clothes and getting on the beers. Things got incredibly lively considering it was a Tuesday night, it turned out that everyone who worked at the Albi just wanted to get drunk, from the Bar Managers to the Chefs, brilliant news. Somewhere during the night, I learnt from Nicole and Joey what a 'Shoey' was. It's quite disgusting to think about sober but when drunk it was very funny. Step 1. Pour your drink into your shoe. Step 2. Drink it out of your shoe. Bear in mind I was pouring a beer into my New Balance trainer that I had worn for the last eight months through shitholes, sweating profusely in them. It did not taste good. We later found that it was easier to do this through a flip-flop/ slider and just pour a drink-through them and use it as a funnel.

Wednesday 2nd August 2017

My first hangover in Weipa was not a nice experience, I could've done with the sun and my bar shift disappearing. Neither did, and a very hungover me walked into the bar at 10 am to be greeted by a knowing Baylee. She was purposely upbeat and loud knowing that I was not in a good place. Baylee wasn't the sort of boss to be angry at me for being hungover at work, she had been there before and understood the pain I was enduring in my stomach and my head. She offered me a Berocca and advised me to order some chips from the kitchen which I did. I don't know what sort of magic is included in a Berocca but I was feeling a lot better and within the hour I was buzzing around the place annoying Baylee and a very hungover Nicole who was not in the mood for my out of tone singing. 'WhEn I wAs SiX YeARs oLd I BroKE mY LeG!'

Friday 4th August 2017

My hair was awful but even awful hair needs cutting. My blonde locks needed dying again and I was due a good skin fade. Cureton's ginger barnet was out of control as well so he was ready for a chop. I had ordered some clippers a couple of weeks before and they had arrived so it was time for us to test our barbering skills in the Common Room. Everything took a long time to get delivered to Weipa as the post came up via boat, I'm still waiting for a pair of

Nike socks to arrive. We cooked Pizza and set up our little barbershop, my turn to cut first. Matt sat a little tentatively in the chair which was completely understandable, I had never cut hair before in my life, how hard could it be?

Quite hard it turned out. I started on a grade three and began trimming his sides, lots was coming off as he had thick hair, jealous. I then moved down to a grade two to give him an attempted fade which was not in any way shape or form a fade. I tried my best to blend it all in but in truth, I butchered his head. 'It'll grow back mate.' I told him as I handed him the mirror. He didn't think it was that bad which made me wonder what on earth his barber back home had been doing to him.

Cureton's turn in the driving seat. My freshly dyed blonde hair was already short so he didn't have too much to do. His method was to get the sides very short and go from there and he did just that. With no grade on the clippers, he went about cutting my hair and lots was coming off the sides and falling to the floor. The end product was me looking like the shittest Peaky Blinder in the world. Short back and stomping had been taken to a whole new level, I looked awful. 'It'll grow back mate!' Cureton laughed.

Wednesday 9th August 2017

The best thing that can happen in Weipa is getting the same day off as a few of your favourite people. That finally happened for me, I had checked the rota and realised that Cureton, Nicole, Corina and Dean all had the day off as well. HWFG! We could've done something productive with our days off, but we decided against that idea immediately and headed to the Bowlies for lunch and some cocktails. The sun was shining and the drinks were flowing, it was the perfect set up for an all-dayer. I knew some of the bar staff at the Bowlies as they had come over to the Albi for all dayers when they had days off. I got extremely jealous standing behind the bar and watching people drink in the sun with their mates so I was extremely happy to be on the better side of the bar.

Dean and Corina were a little drunk and flirty which I called out immediately and it resulted in us trying to set them up together. I was Weipa's answer to Paddy McGuinness. Corina explained that it's not professional to sleep with your boss and I told her she needed to grow up. It must have been incredibly annoying for them both but Nicole, Matt and I were in drunk, immature mode and we weren't letting it go. I had my first spin on the Pokies and turned $10 into $0 which was just great, I had theoretically just bought two schooners and poured them down the drain. *Fun*!

Things escalated from lunchtime cocktails into evening shots and resulted in a stumble back to the Albi at about 8 pm. We made it to the Common Room for another couple of drinks, but we were all worse for wear. I ended up in bed by 10 pm which was perfect, always good to get eight hours or more sleep in!

Friday 11th August 2017

I'd had a relatively busy day at the bar so was ready for comfies and chill in the Common Room with an average film on to fall asleep too. Just as I was about to leave my room I got a knock at my door. It was Jamie and he was there to ask if I would do the pot washing shift that evening. I would've rather it been Ted Bundy at my door. Sean, the regular pot washer and guitar player had left the Albi but the pots still needed washing. I was not a happy man and made it known by having a face like a slapped ass on arrival. Nicole, Jacqui and Vicky all laughed at me and said that I was their bitch for the night which made matters even worse.

During the shift it wasn't the worst thing ever, I was spraying plates and pots clear with a very powerful hose, shoving them in a dishwasher and then putting them all back out, it was pretty tedious but nothing too soul-destroying. It helped that I could have a laugh with Richie and Joey in the kitchen and Nicole and Jacqui who were bringing me plates on bowls on plates. I would've rather been watching a movie, but it wasn't too bad after all. That was until everyone left.

Once the restaurant closed it got a quick wipe down and stock count and then everyone buggered off. The kitchen was the same, they cleared their stations, threw a few more dirty pots my way and were off as well. Then it was just me and a pile of plates and pots. For the next hour and a half, my dignity was removed, thrown on the floor and spat on. I was soaking wet, my feet were freezing and I had food all over me. I finished that shift at 1130 at night and walked up to the bar to grab a coke and sign out for the night. Dean, Deano and Asta told me I stunk and looked awful which I completely agreed with whilst necking a schooner of coke. I showered for extra-long that evening, I have never felt dirtier in my life. Pot washing would be avoided at all costs in the future.

Sunday 13th August 2017

There had been rumours of a Sunday session happening for a while now and finally, it occurred. Those who had the day off were getting on the booze early doors and those who were working would join when they could. I knocked on Nicole's door at 10 am with a bottle of bubbly and some orange juice, we were going to have mimosas for breakfast and get the party started. Bubbly and Orange Juice is as tasty and dangerous a combination as there ever has and ever will be. Once we had sunk a bottle, Matt, Mason and Charmaine De La Rosa from reception joined us and we sat in the beer garden of the Albi all day. A local chap played some live music throughout the day which included every singalong banger that I could think of and the place was buzzing which made it an even better occasion for drinking.

We didn't stay at the Albi all evening as no one who was working needed to see us all drunk having loads of fun so we all wandered over to the Bowlies. Here I was introduced to vodka, lime and water which on paper sounded like sick in a cup. I tried it and I loved it and Nicole informed me that not only would it get me drunk it would hydrate me and ease the hangover. I'm not sure what a scientist would have to say about that, but it seemed legitimate enough for me. I drank vodka, lime and water until I lost the ability to walk and then somehow stumbled home with the other drunk staff members.

The problem was that I didn't stumble back to my room, I accidentally stumbled back to Nicoles and rearranged some furniture with her.

Monday 14th August 2017

We spent the morning laughing at the fact we had just had a bit of jiggery-pokery, it was something that we didn't see coming, excuse the pun. That morning I also called her out on the vodka and water myth, it hurt to open my eyes and everything was triple-bright!

News spread fast around the Albi and a few hours later I had Cureton sat next to me asking a hundred questions as I was trying to enjoy some peaceful Brooklyn 99 in the darkness of the Common Room. Even Eirene, who I called Nana Pat by then because she looked after me like my nan does, came in to give me some shit. I told her I was just helping Nicole with some renovations in her room, I didn't want my Weipa grandma knowing the details.

Thursday 17th August 2017

Remember at the start of the Weipa section I told you about the alcoholic beverage named Divas? It's the stuff that kills a brain cell per sip. I had purchased a bottle of the strawberry flavour and a bottle of lemonade and was ready to get sideways. Dean Furber (just in case you have forgotten) had the day off as well and had decided that he wanted to spend it getting drunk with me, an excellent plan from him I must admit. Dean had been pretty sensible since arriving but had now established himself as a reliable bloke so was ready to let his hair down. Come under my wing Dean and I will show you the way.

We made our way over to the Bowlies where I fed him the same bullshit that Nicole had fed me a few nights before. 'Let's get on the voddy lime and water, it'll help the hangover tomorrow.' I lied to his face. Dean didn't mind the sound of that and suggested that we made them doubles. We both knew this was a bad life decision but we ran with it! We watched sport, bet on the horses, drank vodka and lost on the pokies all day, it was brilliant. Just as we began to peak I whispered the dreaded words that no one wants to hear in Dean's left ear. 'I've got Divas at the Albi.' Like the drunken idiots that we were, we jumped in a taxi for the two-minute drive to the Albi and I made myself and Dean our first-ever Divas and lemonade. For a brief moment, it wasn't bad and I could taste the strawberry, then the aftertaste hit me and it tasted like flavoured hand sanitiser. We couldn't not drink the whole bottle though I had paid all of $12 for it. We ran out of lemonade quickly and come the end of the bottle were just drinking Divas on the rocks, we were even swirling it round like it was an expensive whisky.

The night ended with Nicole and Corina coming over to witness what can only be described as the worst dad dancing to ever happen by Dean and me, we were so drunk, Divas had destroyed the majority of our brain cells. I drunkenly told Corina and Dean it was about time they got it on to which sober Corina told me to piss off. I then told Nicole that we should get it on and she put me to bed. Good call.

Saturday 26th August 2017

DJ Mason was playing live at the Albi, put your hands up in the air! Sadly, for me I would not be putting my hands up as I would be working, you know that thing that I was in Weipa to do? I had worked in the Drive-Thru in the morning so was already knackered come the start of the DJ Mason set at 9 pm. It turned out Mason was a pretty popular DJ in Weipa, the Albi was packed with people all dancing terribly, flirting badly and getting drunk, I was beyond jealous! I had gotten to know a few of the locals over the last couple of months which meant they would try and get me to give them a double instead of a single or not charge them for the mixer. If I really liked them I would not charge for the mixer but this was mainly reserved for Albi staff members and the Bowlies staff who were often kind enough to not charge me for a dash of coke in a spiced rum.

This was without question the busiest I had seen the bar. Everyone that could work was working and it still felt hectic. I made my first proper cock up behind the bar in the rush of it all and dropped an entire bottle of Bundaberg Red on the floor resulting in it smashing into a million pieces. A single Bundy Red and coke was $5 so I had just dropped around $150 worth of alcohol on the floor, very cool. Understandably Jamie looked at me like he was going to rip my throat out.

Once everyone had stumbled out for their after-parties and one-night stands it was just me, Asta and Deano clearing tables and making sure everything was counted and ready for the morning. Deano pulled us all a schooner and we went and sat outside for 20 minutes and chatted utter rubbish. I didn't get the chance to talk to Asta as much because she didn't live at the Albi and I only ever saw her at work so it was good to chew the fat off a few things. She was openly a gamer nerd and she also threw back a schooner before I could even take a sip of mine. Every single man in Weipa came into the bar and tried their luck with Asta, every night she would be approached by a man and sometimes even a woman and would get an ear full of some awful chat up lines. She told me some of them and I noted them down for future use, they have not been successful.

Tuesday 5th September 2017
Agreeing to an early morning gym session was immediately regretted as I had a very energetic Cureton knocking on my door at 8 am. That's right, we joined a gym, unbelievable I know. I dragged myself up and got myself changed and was out the door by five past. He thought that it would be a good idea for us to run to the gym, I disagreed, running is the work of the devil and I hate it with every ounce of my being. He told me I was scared because I knew that he would be better at running than me. Luckily, reverse psychology only works on idiots.

We ran to the gym and I nearly died on route, it was unbearably hot and after all that Matt beat me comfortably. What a waste of time.

Pig Valve Malfunction

On Friday 8th September I had some chest pains throughout my shift at the Drive-Thru. I initially put this down to pulling a muscle lifting a crate or something similar so just continued as normal. As the shift progressed my chest got tighter and it became more difficult to breathe, I was pretty certain it wasn't a heart attack so I wasn't overly worried about it. After a solid hour or so of pains, I informed Dean of the situation as he was working in the Drive-Thru with me and he was pretty sure I should get it checked out, so that's what I did. As expected, Weipa hospital is relatively small and certainly did not have a specialist cardiac unit to check me over.

The ECG results came back abnormal, I explained to the doctor that this was always the case due to a leaky valve that I had replaced yet still leaks a little bit, the little bugger. He didn't feel comfortable with just taking my word for it and called down to Townsville, the nearest hospital with a specialist cardiology ward for a second opinion. Their opinion was that I needed to be seen pretty quickly at their hospital as they didn't like the look of the ECG recording either. This was not ideal. The only way for me to get from Weipa to Townsville in decent time was to fly it so they sent up a medical aeroplane to Weipa Airport and I was escorted via ambulance to the plane. I'll be honest at this stage I was panicking a little bit, maybe the pig valve had finally had enough of my poor treatment of it over the previous seven years.

The flight to Townsville was surreal, I was in a plane that was also a hospital, it had two doctors and all the equipment needed should an emergency occur. The doctor put some drugs in me that made me talk gibberish for a few minutes and then was sound asleep. I arrived in Townsville Hospital in the early hours and the initial Doctors were also worried about my test results. It wasn't until the Senior Consultant came in on Saturday morning that someone understood what was going on. We talked about my background and he informed me that the valve itself was leaking but not to an extent that would require any surgery. He wanted to keep me in for 24-hour observations just to be extra safe, but he was sure it was not an emergency. He also sent his thoughts across to Tony, my consultant in Southampton, so he could have his very important say on proceedings

24 hours of worrying later and I was able to leave the hospital which was a huge relief. I am aware that my valve will need replacing again but was extremely thankful that it didn't happen whilst enjoying myself in Australia. I was informed to take it easy and not overexert in the gym for the foreseeable and I assured the consultant that that wouldn't be a problem at all!

Wednesday 20th September 2019

Over the last week, everyone had been rushing around like blue-arsed flies making sure that everything was in place for the arrival of Bill who was the owner of the resort. I met Bill on my way to my bar shift and he seemed very nice, he told me that he didn't mind Poms because his late wife was one. Everyone acted differently whilst Bill was there, it was all much more professional, and everyone had their tails between their legs.

Bill had brought Jane along with him who was the Director of the business, she was born in England but had lived in Australia for so long that she had lost her accent. I liked Jane immediately because the first thing she did was order a double whisky with a splash of coke to accompany her lunch and stuck it straight on Bill's tab.

For the next three days, everyone was extra nice to customers and Deano spoke completely differently, he had gone from bogan to upper-class at the blink of an eye. The same Deano that was usually shouting at the TV for a horse to 'Fuckin' kick on!!' was now advising people that the house red was very fruity. I told him to cut the act and stop being such an ass licker. He checked that no one important was in earshot and called me a cunt five times in a 20-second outburst. He needed it, I could tell that he had been holding it all in.

Monday 23rd September 2017

Some celebrity guests arrived at the Albi and I initially didn't recognise any of them, I didn't know of any Australian celebrities really so I was hoping for Kylie Minogue at best and Tim Cahill at worst. It wasn't until I heard their surname as they booked their table for dinner later on that it all clicked into place, it was the Irwin family. If you don't know who Steve Irwin is then chances are you are either too young to be reading this book or you hate animals. Steve Irwin was one of my favourite people growing up, I liked him as much as I liked David Beckham and Dick and Dom In Da Bungalow. He was a legend and it was an incredibly sad day when he died.

His wife and kids were carrying on his legacy and are all still heavily involved in the preservation of land for animals to roam freely as well as owning a large Zoo near Brisbane. I had seen a few videos on YouTube of Steve's children holding snakes and other horrible animals that scare me. The kids, Bindi and Robert and their mum Terri were all very polite and smiley, maybe a touch too smiley if you ask me. I refrained from telling them how much I loved their dad and ex-husband before that bastard stingray killed him. They weren't huge celebrities to me so I wasn't overly excited unlike most of the staff at the Albi. There were plenty of selfies and signings happening. The Irwins are still a very big deal in Australia and every man of a certain age thought that Terri, the mum, was smoking hot. It was difficult to disagree with them. I wish that stingray didn't kill Steve because if he had walked into the bar, I would've gone full fangirl and lost my shit!

Tuesday 26th September 2017
It was time to start planning for the future as I wasn't going to be in Weipa forever and needed to be in Melbourne for Christmas as we would be watching the Boxing Day Test and a few friends from university were coming over. Chevs and I had kept in touch since my swift exit from Tolga, he had managed to complete his farm work and was now working and living in Sydney the lucky sod. He had got so drunk one night that he got a £200 cab to meet a girl that he had been talking to on tinder which resulted in zero sex and him passing out on her sofa. So he hadn't changed. We both wanted to travel the East Coast of Australia ideally by car so we did a little bit of research

on how to go about this. The most sensible idea was renting a camper van and stopping off at different campsites on the way down the coast, this would save us money on hostels although it would cost us money in van rental. The other option was for me to buy a van/truck in Weipa, drive it to Cairns to meet Chevs and then drive the East Coast before selling it at the end. This way we wouldn't lose much money as the truck shouldn't lose too much value as long as we didn't crash it. Chevs had already crashed a motorbike twice on our travels so I was slightly tentative about the idea of him driving me around in a truck.

After a very sensible discussion by mine and Chevs's standards, we decided that I would buy a truck in Weipa and drive it down to meet him in Cairns at the start of December. The big risk was not being able to sell the car at the end of the trip, but I could always leave it in Sydney and wait for it to sell and get Chevs to transfer me over the money. A flawless plan I am sure you will agree. We ended the FaceTime and I got straight on to the Weipa buy and sell Facebook page for a search. It was like the Dark Web, if I was in the market for a gun, a fishing rod or a large knife I would have been in luck! What I was in the market for was something big, cheap and ideally working.

Monday 2nd October 2017

October already?! The time was flying in Weipa. I had found a car on Facebook and it was in my price range. It was as basic as it gets, a big, white Toyota Land Cruiser that had seen better days with over 200,000 kilometres on the clock. Everything about this car screamed yes to me. It was massive, had lots of room for luggage and sleeping and it had a huge speaker in the back for me to blare some rubbish music down the coast. It had an asking price of $4000 which was dangerously reasonable. At that price there was going to be some problems with it, I just prayed they happened with the next owner and not me. It was a lot of car for the money and the worst-case scenario was that I sold it for scraps for about $1000. I must have had my big boy pants on at the time because I shook hands there and then on this battered old Toyota. $4000 down and the owner of a new truck, I sent a picture to Chevs and he loved it too, we had our East Coast wagon and I named him Reginald II. Nana Pat grabbed a sponge and we gave the old car a deep clean both inside and out, once it had been cleaned it didn't look half as old and crap.

Wednesday 3rd October 2017

Reginald II wasn't going to spend his time in Weipa parked up, I wanted to go and test the old boy out with some off-roading and beach driving. Cureton was free and keen to come for a drive and was also a very good DJ playing constant bangers on this little excursion. There didn't seem to be any problems driving off-road which was very important. One thing that was noticeable when driving it for a longer period was how uncomfortable and hot it became. There was no air conditioning and the seats were leather which meant they were like sitting on an open fire. The road from Weipa to Cairns is 820km of dust tracks and potholes and would take me over 20 hours to complete, all of a sudden buying a car here didn't seem like the best idea ever. In for a penny in for a pound.

Wednesday 11th October 2017

Tony and Vicki were going on an away trip to a nice lake about an hour outside of Weipa and invited Joey and me to join. In typical incest, Weipa style Tony and Vicki were now also lovering each other. Tony was a seasoned off-roader and loved a fish so I agreed to join as long as I could follow him out. Joey joined as he also loved fishing and the fact that he wasn't driving meant that he could drink plenty of beer on his day off.

The roads were a little more challenging than the ones I had taken on with Matt a couple of days earlier. They were much bumpier and the route involved driving over fallen trees and through lakes which I wasn't a massive fan of. Toyota's were said to be indestructible so I just had to trust that Reginald would make his way through the river and not get swept away leading to the deaths of Joey and I. The old boy passed the test with flying colours and we arrived at the lake and opened a crate of warm beers, crap. Tony was much more prepared than I was, he had fridges, air-con and stuff in his 4x4, a very handy piece of kit in the skin melting heat of Far North Queensland.

I am not one for fishing and I wasn't about to pretend that I enjoyed it at all. The thought of chucking a line out into the water and waiting for a fish to have a nibble on some bait appealed to me about as much as peeling my toenails off. But I went along with Joey and Tony who loved it. It was pretty peaceful sitting on the side of the lake having a beer and soaking up some Vitamin D. Relaxing until there was a fish on the line and Tony would go into full mentalist mode until it was flapping about on the floor next to him. The only thing that's pleasing about fishing was the result when it was cooked and served with some chips.

Joey and I had to make our way back as Tony and Vicki would be staying in the love shack by the lake for the night. Drunk Joey assured me that he knew the way back and I had no choice but to trust him. On the way home, he told me a story about how he and another chap had got lost on the way home once and ran out of petrol, an episode that nearly resulted in their deaths. 'Yo, I was seeing things, man, my mind was playing tricks on my eyes, I could see cars coming towards me and then they'd just disappear,' he explained. Suddenly I trusted him a lot less.

Sunday 22nd October 2017

Shit Shirt Sippy Cup Sunday. Baylee had gifted me a sippy cup designed for a baby a few weeks earlier because I was a child after a few drinks which is an accurate description of me. I drank Morgan Spiced and Coke through the sippy cup from midday until midnight, a proper all-dayer in which most people got involved at some stage. Even Jamie joined for a pint at lunchtime, I had been annoying him for weeks about joining in, 'You might even have some fun.' I would say to his ever-expressionless face.

I ended up at Nicole's for kick-ons* that night and we drank until the early hours of Monday morning. We were both in absolutely no shape to perform any rumpy-pumpy and both fell asleep fully clothed. Then everything went Pete Tong.

*Kick-ons are when everyone else has called it a night but you find a second wind and go again! This can also happen in the morning if you wake up with a hangover and crack open a cold beer you are kicking on.

Monday 23rd October 2017

A day that will be etched into my mental history book forever. I woke up fully clothed in Nicole's bed and had given myself a golden shower. This was not ok. That half an hour of lying there waiting for Nicole to wake up and give me a bollocking felt like an eternity. I was staring at the ceiling debating whether leaving Weipa immediately was the best option. When she eventually woke, I took a deep breath and told her the news.

'I've wet your bed.' Laughter, and lots of it. Nicole couldn't stop laughing at the fact I had wet her bed. 'Go and get the cleaning stuff, you child.' She laughed me right out of her room. It had gone a lot better than I expected but I still felt disgusting. I walked to my room, got showered and changed and then proceeded to get the cleaning stuff from the common room to take to Nicole's.

Thud! A brief wonder what had made that noise followed by searing pain starting in my big toe and spreading through my whole body. I whispered fuck as loud as I could, that makes sense, doesn't it? I looked down at my right foot. There was blood everywhere pouring out of my big toe, I had stubbed it so hard on the steps it had resulted on my toenail bending back and pretty much coming off. I can still feel it now looking back at it and it makes my toes curl. I hobbled into Nicole's room and told her what had happened and then realised that I was now bleeding all over her floor. I couldn't deal with my life at that stage, I had wet a bed that wasn't even mine to wet, I had stubbed my big toenail almost off and I was dealing with a huge hangover on a couple of hours sleep. I needed turning off and on, I looked at her like the broken man I was and she told me to stop fucking bleeding on the floor. I grabbed a blanket from the Common Room, wrapped my foot up and we both fell asleep on the floor for the next four hours. When I woke up my toe hurt a thousand times more and I now had to clean both the floor and the bed. It was quite easy for everyone to find out about my little accident on Nicole's bed as we had to put the mattress outside to air off and dry and everyone could see it. I would never live this down.

Wednesday 1st November 2017

I had been on my best behaviour over the last week or so, I hadn't touched a drop of alcohol. I was hobbling around like an idiot due to my toe being strapped up, anyone would've thought my foot had been bitten off by an alligator. I didn't dare to pull the toenail that so desperately wanted to come off, off. After a week of being off the booze, I was long overdue a good Common Room session with everyone. This wasn't something that I had suggested but I didn't need much persuading from Cureton at all. A few people would be leaving over the coming months so it was important to make the most of these rare times we all had an evening off.

Nana Pat, being the arty-farty creative human that she is, created us some headbands that she had made out of an old dress that she no longer wanted. Headband Wednesdays had a pretty good ring to it so we all decided that this would become a weekly thing until we left. I had upgraded from Divas as I was pretty sure the stuff was causing permanent damage to my vital organs, I was now a gin drinker, how very civilised.

Things went from 0-60 quick and Cureton and I ended up in Nicole's room for kick ons yet again once everyone had gone to bed. These kick ons didn't stop, this was the first and only time I have ever genuinely had no sleep at all which was not ideal because I was working my first breakfast shift that morning.

Thursday 2nd November 2017

As expected, the no-sleep breakfast shift was excruciatingly painful. I got lucky and was doing it with Milo who was relatively new and brilliant at making coffee with fancy stuff on the top. If a customer wanted some swirls on the top of their latte Milo was the person to go to. I could cock up a cup of tea so I was more than happy to leave the hot drinks to her. Thankfully it was quiet and Joey was the breakfast chef which meant a sneaky bit of bacon here and there to keep me going. How I didn't faint I do no know. I clearly looked bad as when Vicki came in to set up for lunch, she told me that I looked like shit and reeked of booze. I made it back to my room, showered and fell into bed at 11 am. I didn't wake up until 10 pm that evening completely ruining whatever body clock I had left.

Saturday 11th November 2017

It was a sad day in Weipa because Baylee was leaving us. She was off to start her new life and family with her boyfriend and no one could blame her. She ensured that as many of us as possible had the day off so we could get our drink on. Jamie was hosting us at his house for a BBQ and drinks, we were under strict instructions to not be hammered by the time we arrived there, afterwards, we had full permission to let ourselves go which was never going to end well.

The BBQ was incredible, I ate so much chicken and coleslaw whilst drinking lots of Morgan Spiced and Coke through my sippy cup. Jane had come up for the leaving party as well and I was extremely happy to see that she was drinking whisky like it was water. I tried my very best to persuade Jamie to come over to the Common Room for afters, but his willpower was too strong. Jane needed far less persuading, she was asking me when we could all go and get this party started.

There is something quite brilliant about getting drunk with your boss. It is the same feeling when you see your old teachers at the pub and realise that they are just humans that need a glass of wine now and then too. That night I was getting drunk with my boss and my bosses' boss. Everyone was on the same level after a skin-full of alcohol, I have seen some awful dancing in my time, but I think Jane's shapes were the worst and she didn't care at all. It was a fitting farewell to Baylee who had made my time in Weipa a lot more bearable. She had saved me with hundreds of Berocca and for that, I am forever in her debt.

Tuesday 14th November 2017

Every new beginning comes from some other beginnings' end or something like that. I handed my notice into Jamie who was expecting it as I had spoken with him about where to visit whilst travelling down the East Coast. He'd never admit it, but I could see in his eyes that he was sad I was leaving. I was like an annoying nephew to him, but I was also a half-decent worker. I could do everything from pot-washing against my will to pulling schooners to taking two plates from the kitchen to a table without dropping them. I could even be extra nice to customers if I got told they were important. I was just as sad to be leaving myself. Weipa had become a home from home for me, I had made some really good friends and everything was in a nice routine. I was also extremely excited though, as in a couple of weeks I would be setting off to Cairns to meet Chevs in what was sure to be the piss-up of the century.

Friday 17th November 17

I had learnt to expect the unexpected in Weipa but even I was surprised by the events of Friday 17th November. I had friendly flirtations with Jacqui throughout my time in Weipa but got nowhere and expected nothing for my efforts. Mason, the very handsome and muscular man that he is, had dated her before I had arrived, but they had a lover's quarrel a couple of months earlier and were no longer mating.

A few of us went across to Kodie's house, one of our friends from outside of work, for many beers that evening, it was more of a house party than casual beers. Her house was very busy and I sat on the kitchen counter boshing cans of beer. Jacqui and I were good mates by this stage so when the party came to a close due to some neighbours complaining we started the 20-minute walk back to the Albi. Somewhere between Kodie's and the Albi we had a little kiss ended up getting a little bit frisky. Being the open man that I am, I asked Jacqui if I was going to see her in her birthday suit to which she nodded, how this was happening I do not know but it was.

We got back to the Albi, went into her room and Marvin Gaye got it on. Then things got even crazier. A drunk Mason opened Jacqui's window from the outside and started climbing through like Jack Nicholson in The Shining. *Heeeere's Mason!* As he poked his face through the curtains he was greeted by my pale backside. There were a few seconds of silence which felt like a lifetime before Mason laughed and wiggled his way back through the window and closed it up. What the hell had just happened?! Once our bedroom rodeo was over Jacqui and I worked out that Mason had probably popped over for a little drunk booty call and was not expecting to see me there. My drunk brain couldn't process it all at the time, my sober brain struggled for days afterwards. Weipa is the fucking Catalina Wine Mixer.

Wednesday 22nd November 2017

My last headband Wednesday. I was in a nice drunk mood and told everyone present how much I loved them which was true. Asta joined us in the Common Room which was a rare event for her because she could just go home which was much more comfortable for her however, she made an exception for my last Wednesday night session. I had drunk many shots with Asta on our random nights out over the last few months and was fully aware she could drink me under the table no problem. When she arrived with three bottles of wine I knew that I was plugged in for the long haul.

As everyone sloped off to bed me and Asta drank the largest glasses of red wine and watched endless amounts of Brooklyn 99. We completely lost track of time amongst quoting Big Shaq's – Man's Not Hot and laughing at Brooklyn 99 and were shocked to see Milo walking past on the way to her breakfast shift. 'Fuccck that's six o'clock mate, I've got work in three hours. Love you byeeeee.' Asta was up and off on the short walk home. I fell asleep immediately on the couch only to be woken up by an energetic Nicole jumping about the place and blending some fruit with the worlds loudest blender, there was no rest for the wicked.

Monday 27th November 2017

Nate decided that it would be a good idea to go clay pigeon shooting which sounded like a lot of fun to me. We rallied the troops and eight of us headed off to the shooting range. I had never fired a gun and am awful at Call of Duty so had no expectations of being any good. The chap doing the demonstration made it look exceptionally easy which gave me confidence that I might hit a few. I picked up the gun and concentrated as hard as I could. 'Paul!' I shouted at the bloke whose name was Gary. He released the clay pigeon and I shot the gun missing it by a good 20 feet. Just a few pre-match nerves, let's give that another go. 'Paul!' Target acquired, gun pointing right at it, trigger pulled, missed by a mile again. This was very difficult.

What made this even more frustrating was the fact that everyone was stepping up and shooting clay pigeons out of the sky like they were John Wayne. Had they been sneakily coming to the range for practice all this time? I proceeded to shoot at the clay pigeons 30 times and didn't hit a single one. I finished bottom of the leader board comfortably, the next worse score was five. Gary asked if I wanted a print out of the leader board and I told him that he better watch his mouth or I'd shoot him. He told me I would miss.

Saturday 2nd December 2017

Just like that, I had worked my last shift at the Albi and was a free man again. My last shift was in the bar with Dean, Deano, Asta and Nicole which was the dream team. I finished early and got a schooner on the house which was a nice touch and set me up for the evening's activities nicely. Of course, the last Saturday I spent in Weipa was going to be spent getting drunk.

I invited every Tom, Dick and Harry that I liked to the Bowls Club for one last night on the vodka, lime and water and hopefully a few lucky spins on the pokies. Corina had purchased me a horrendous beige suit from the local charity shop and insisted that I wore it which I obliged to. I looked like a very boring, lesbian supply teacher.

Once the Bowlies closed I invited a few back with all of us for more booze at the Common Room. There were strict rules that no one other than staff members could drink in there but I had already left the job, they couldn't sack me. Dean and Deano were waiting for my return as they had been working but like the good blokes that they are, wanted to have a farewell drink with me. I drank until I could drink no more, Asta told me to stop being a little bitch but I had to concede that on this occasion I was one. I passed out on the sofa at 3 am, Weipa/Asta had finally defeated me at the last.

Monday 4th December 2017

It was time to hit the road. I had somehow persuaded Joey to come down with me for a few nights out in Cairns and then fly back up. He was more than happy to do this as long as we stayed at Gilligans which of course we were. What was this mythical place that everyone spoke so highly of? Monday consisted mainly of putting my life back into my backpack. It was nice to have some wardrobe space and a double bed for a few months, I was going to miss that hugely. Shit shirts, swimming trunks, hair clippers and a pair of jeans later my rucksack was full to the brim again.

Richie had kindly given my car a quick service in the hope that it didn't break down on the 480-mile road from Weipa to Cairns, I bought him a crate of beer for his troubles which he appreciated. Out of the kitchen, Richie was a great bloke, in the kitchen he was very angry and scary. I had decided that we would leave in the evening so we could get as much of the trip done whilst it was a bit cooler at night, there was no working air-conditioning in Reginald II so driving in the heat wasn't going to be as enjoyable as a Mrs Browns Boys marathon.

7 pm came around and that was my cue to leave. I packed my car up and hugged goodbye to my Weipa family and was genuinely sad about this. As I drove off into the darkness, I reflected on what had been an unexpectedly amazing chapter in my life. The community of Weipa and the Albatross Bay Resort had welcomed me with open arms and made my stay far better than I had ever imagined it being. I

had made some friends for life in Cureton, Nicole, Asta, Corina and double Deans. I still keep in touch with Nicole, Asta and Cureton to this day and am happy to report that they are still all absolutely bonkers. Asta even popped over to the UK during her European travels and I met her in London for a load of pints, not pathetic schooners. She still drank me under the table effortlessly. Until we meet again Weipa you hot, silly place.

Tony

Sadly, whilst writing this book Tony passed away whilst out on his boat. RIP Tone. A great chef and a genuinely top bloke.

The East Coast

Tuesday 5th December 2017

The drive from Weipa to Cairns took a back and anus-destroying 21 hours which may seem like a long time, and it was but was a pretty good effort from Joey and me. It is far too long to spend in any car let alone a shitty old Toyota but somehow it went quite quickly, a mixture of excitement and napping helped me along the way. We took shifts behind the wheel which gave us both a chance to get some shut-eye, in total I would say I slept for two hours tops. The road itself was incredibly bumpy most of the way, irrigation I think they called it, which meant that the rare comfortable position that I got into was soon ruined by a large bump in the road shaking me awake. As we arrived in Cairns I was running on fumes and had no more strawberry pencils to eat. Reginald II hadn't missed a beat the whole way, the old boy flew down eating up potholes and spitting them back out. The huge speaker came in handy after 18 hours of driving when it was broad daylight, scorching hot and neither of us could get the sleep that we so desperately needed, we just cranked up the music and left us with no option but to stay awake. Joey's music taste was very different to mine, I was blaring some Oasis and Arctic Monkeys whereas he was blaring some old school Tupac and Eminem.

There isn't much I would drive 21 hours for, dinner with Michelle Keegan perhaps, but meeting up with Benjamin Cheverells was one of those reasons. I parked up in Gilligans car park and checked into the hostel room that Chevs had booked us all in too. It was five o'clock in the afternoon so I chucked my bag in the room knowing full well Chevs was going to be somewhere near the bar. I walked out to the pool area and was greeted by the eighth wonder of the world, Chevs in the sun with a schooner having had about 12 already. I embraced Chevs like Davina McCall had just introduced me to my long-lost brother and told him how much I had missed him. All drunk Chevs could say back to me was 'Yesss Bouch, haha. Yes, Bouch!' Which I knew was his way of telling me he missed me too. I introduced him to Joey and he introduced me to the two lads he had been drinking with all day, Derek and Kev. That's the last you'll hear of them, they were a pair of bucket-hat wearing nonces.

The next few hours were spent trying to get on the same level as Chevs, this meant having a spiced rum chaser with every schooner. Tuesday was bingo night at Gilligans, I was fairly sure this wasn't an event for the local oldies and would get extremely lively. I went back to the room for a much-needed shower and change of clothes before heading down to get involved. We gained a Portuguese girl from our hostel room who was also keen to come and get drunk, everyone else in the room declined our offer, dull as dishwater. Who stays at Gilligans and has a night in? Fun sponges, that's who. Bingo was, if anything, too lively, every number meant a drink of some sort and if you had a line (a bingo line not the other kind) or a full house you would win some money but also have to do a dirty pint. People were on the tables and Gilligans was wall-to-wall with backpackers and stag-dos. I could already see why it was rated so highly by everyone I had spoken to about Cairns.

The night ended up elsewhere in Cairns, I couldn't tell you what bar we just stumbled in there and stayed until we couldn't stand up anymore. Being extremely drunk and tired at the same time is a very strange feeling, my head was telling me to get a shot in and hit the dance floor, but my body was telling me to get to bed, you idiot! Eventually, I had to listen to my body and as soon as my head hit the pillow I was out like a light. Rest was important and needed because I was going to do it all again tomorrow.

Wednesday 6th December 2017

The best/ most dangerous thing about Gilligans is the pool bar that you can buy alcohol at all day. If used correctly you can have a nice relaxing day in the sun with a couple of cold beers to keep hydrated. If used stupidly you could end up drunk in the sun by the early afternoon. Of course, Chevs, Joey and I had chosen option two for the day and were tipsy by three o'clock. We were then joined by Rueben who was a chap I met whilst in Weipa, he was originally from the UK but had lived in Australia for a long while. He was a Cairns regular so knew the different bars and clubs that we needed to go to for a good time on a Wednesday. That night we would also be meeting up with Mason who now lived and worked in Cairns since leaving the Albi a week before me. If my memory serves me correctly he had punched a hole in his door after a few too many beers, I'm not sure what led him to do this...

Rueben informed us that Gilligans was not the place to be on a Wednesday night which came as a shock to me as I assumed it was always the place to be. Throughout the day it certainly was the pool and bar were both rammed. It made me feel a lot better being a little drunk at three in the afternoon because so was everyone else in this hostel. One girl was sick on herself after attempting to down a drink and failing spectacularly, she was carried to her room at 4 pm, not a great effort. Cotton Club was the location of choice for tonight, but we were going to have a decent bar crawl beforehand to see all of Cairns best attractions. One of these attractions was the bar that Mason now worked in which was for those that were part of the high society of Cairns. We snuck in for one discounted cocktail that I had to get a mortgage for and Mason clocked out and joined in the madness.

Cotton Club was a very good bar for a few reasons but mainly because you could get on the tables and dance. Getting on a table sober would never cross my mind. I would be terrified of falling off and breaking my neck. After a day on the beer, it seemed like the best thing in the world to me despite it being more likely for me to fall to my death.

Friday 8th December 2017

Sadly, Chevs and I had to leave Gilligans and Cairns after just one or two more beers else we would have spiralled out of control and would still be there now. Even if you read this in 2027 that is still a realistic statement. Gilligans had lived up to all expectations, the place was a hostel for daft and the drunk and I was both of those things throughout. Cairns is lucky to have such a good hostel because without it there wouldn't be many reasons to visit as a backpacker. Before leaving Cairns the next day I had to pop Reginald II to a mechanic because he was leaking a bit of oil. I say a little bit, there was a good-sized swimming pool of oil underneath the old truck. No dramas at all and it was fixed within a couple of minutes. I must admit when I went up to the car and saw it had taken a leak all over the floor my heart was in my ass, I was prepared for engine failure or something just as drastic. Just a $20 bung thankfully.

We needed to give Gilligans and Cairns the send-off that it thoroughly deserved. This was made very easy as the hostel was hosting a sangria and trivia night from 8 pm. I had only ever had sangria once before in Magaluf 2012 on my first lads holiday and I ended up in a tattoo parlour getting a four-leafed clover tattooed on my right quadricep. Some things never change, that night I sipped sangria through a straw for two hours and ended up struggling to hold normal conversations with anyone. Cotton Club was even better after a few jugs of rocket fuel, I was on the tables until the early am, as was Chevs.

Saturday 9th December
It was one of those days where I just wanted to stay in bed flicking through Netflix and eating takeaways. This was not an option though, as Chevs and I had to make the trip down to Airlie Beach where we would be staying for the next few days. At this stage, I was quite annoyed with Australia for being so unnecessarily big! I had already driven 480 miles to get to Cairns, now I had to get back in my Toyota LandOven and drive it 385 miles to Airlie Beach. Everything was so far away! The only plus was that the roads were now smooth highways and not bumpy, dusty lanes meaning that the drive was only going to take about seven hours on a good day. I bid farewell to Joey who was staying another two nights in Gilligans because apparently, a three-day bender wasn't enough before he headed back to Weipa. I hopped in the driver's seat for trip number two.

Not leaving until midday was a mistake, we soon realised that the seven-hour trip was more likely to be nine in my old Land Cruiser, it wasn't the quickest. Nine hours is a lot of time to spend behind the wheel so Chevs and I did shifts, I would drive and he would DJ then vice versa. We had a lot to catch up on so we chatted utter rubbish the entire way down to Airlie Beach. We arrived at 9 pm and there was a little treat waiting for us in one of the local bars. I parked up on the side of the road, Chevs and I were sleeping in the car for the first time that night which was going to be an experience, to say the least. A campsite would've been ideal but a roadside would have to do that night. We went to the bar to be greeted by the crazy Scots Dean, Elliot and Andy! HWFG!

All I had eaten that day was a bacon roll and a meal-deal in the car, I needed something substantial in me before drinking with them. This was not happening, Dean got the first round in and then that was that I was locked in a round for as long as I could bear it. They had been joined by another crazy Scotsman, Tam, who had replaced silly Gavin who was back home. There was only one way this night was going to end and that was in a slump in the back of my car. It was so good to see the Scots but I knew the impact it was going to have on my body and my soul. I have no idea what time I got back to the car, or how I did, my last memory was sending a photo to Gavin with our middle fingers up captioned 'Piss off Gavin, Miss you xx.'

Sunday 10th December 2017

I have said a couple of times in this book; 'this was the worst day of my life,' but this really was the worst day of my life, the Crème Dela Crème of shit days. I had set up a bed in the boot of the car which was just a couple of old duvets from the Albi, one to lie on and one to cover me. I had tested this out in Weipa and it was pretty comfy although a little bit cramped and very hot. When I woke up that morning my boot doors were open, they opened up like a set of French Doors, and my legs were hanging out the back. It was so early the streetlights were still on, I was still incredibly drunk and no one was around. Overnight disaster had struck and will explain why this was the worst day of my life.

There is no easy way to say this, overnight I had done a number two in my shorts in the back of my car. The diet of alcohol, strawberry laces and meal-deals had taken its toll and the schooners with the Scots the night before had tipped me over the edge. I have never been so embarrassed and disgusted with myself in all my life, a fully-grown man shitting himself in the back of his car that is parked up on the side of the road with its back doors open. I was muttering to myself 'you are fucking disgusting, ohh good god, you horrible thing!' I couldn't just sit in my faeces all morning, I needed to go and clean myself up which was going to prove difficult as the motor didn't have an en-suite funnily enough. I climbed out of the car and waddled down to the changing rooms of the swimming pool about 200 metres away which thankfully had a shower. Talk about a walk of shame. I peeled my clothes off and washed so thoroughly it hurt my skin before walking back to the car in just a towel, an all-time low. Chevs was still asleep in the front of the car when I returned, he wasn't going to like my morning story when he woke up.

'In this car?! You are disgusting! Have you washed?' Chevs was disappointed in me for the first time in our friendship. He had finally found his limit with me, I wouldn't have blamed him for just leaving me in Airlie Beach and making his own way down the East Coast. Luckily one of the duvets had taken the hit so there was no human poo in the car itself as I had wedged the duvet in the nearest bin. I couldn't justify my actions to Chevs, we just led in silence and occasionally muttered 'for fuck sake' before eventually just laughing at the state of my life. There we were, led in a car on Airlie Beach that had been used as a toilet overnight by its owner with hangovers hand-delivered by Satan himself. 'It doesn't get any worse than this.' I said out loud. I certainly hoped it didn't.

We needed to get ourselves into a hostel for a good night's sleep else we weren't going to make it any further. We did just that, I showered again, ate a square meal and slept my sins away that night.

Monday 11th – Wednesday 13th December 2017

There is no rest for the wicked. Chevs and I were off on 'The Clipper' which is a boat tour to Whitsundays. Even the Scots had told us that this boat was mental which worried me hugely, they didn't think me pooing the car was mental. I had read some reviews about the boat and it was confirmed to be a big, floating nut-house full of alcohol and sexual activities. We picked up a few boxes of goon and some spirits before heading off to set sail on the tour. Looking back everything just blurs into one so chronological order is not going to be correct here, I was intoxicated for two days straight.

The one person on board that was even drunker than I was for the entire trip was my good friend Benny Chevs, he became a bit of a legend during his time on the boat. He stumbled and bounced around the place for the entire trip unable to speak and consumed so much goon it hurt me to think about it.

There were a lot of people to meet and names to remember so I came up with a very efficient method to ensure I didn't get anyone's name wrong, I called them all Dave. The main Dave's were Canadian Dave whose real name was Ryan, Dr Dave whose real name was Evan and Irish Dave whose real name was Niamh. It was a flawless system and I was called Dave by them as well, so things didn't get confusing. I also met a Canadian and Scottish travel duo Saskia and Amy who were both as mental as one another. Add to that a crazy Irish person named Orlaith and a boat full of people that were ready to get extremely drunk.

Not a whole lot happened on this boat other than drinking and of course, if you get lucky, some afternoon delight. If you don't get lucky on this boat then you are either in a loving relationship, socially awkward or genuinely disgusting to look at. Chevs is a good-looking chap but was dribbling out of the side of his mouth the entire trip and he managed to pull. I was chunky, balding and not overly funky and so did I, that tells you all you need to know about this trip and the standards of everyone on board.

The only downside of the trip was the few top-heavy muscle men who thought they were the best thing since sliced bread and walked around like they owned the boat. All their macho shouting and tensing up wore a bit thin come the end. Thankfully goon had rendered me nearly deaf and blind so they didn't affect me too much once I had a couple of cups of that inside me. The accommodation was the smallest and the worst I had stayed in ever, three people were crammed into a room that could barely fit two. On the last night, most of us slept on the top deck where it was colder but at least we could stretch out.

During this tour, we also visited Whitsundays which is said to be the best beach in the world and my drunken self found it to be as good as any. Chevs saw none of the beach, he passed out on a towel immediately and was woken up as we left.

The Wednesday hangover was as brutal as expected but I can confirm it was not the worst day of my life. The Clipper remains one of the best experiences of my travels, a completely bonkers trip.

Thursday 14th December 2017

Back on the mainland and with a good sleep under our belts, we arranged to meet up with Christina and Dom, two Germans from Tolga Lodge way back when I picked avocados for a living. They were travelling the East Coast as well just in a much more reliable 4x4 than mine with a proper bed in it, it looked comfortable and I was very jealous. They wanted to go to Fraser Island and so did we so it made sense to go together and only take one car. This didn't need a game of rock, paper, scissors, it was clear that Dom's car was the better and safer option to take across to Fraser, it was said to be an off-roading challenge and one that I was certain Reginald II was not up to.

Chevs and I had been lucky throughout our travels and not had to organise anything ourselves. When we were left to organise something it was guaranteed to involve beers. We hit the jackpot again and Christina and Dom organised the entire Fraser Island trip for us, we wouldn't even have to drive, some would say I was chauffeured around.

Friday 15th – Sunday 17th December 2017

This was the only regret of my East Coast trip. Fraser Island itself was a lovely spot but we should've done a tour. People had mentioned that Fraser could be as lively as The Clipper if you went with the right group and that was something that I missed out on. It was still a great trip, but it was more of a relaxing getaway than it was anything else. I didn't meet anyone new, I didn't get silly drunk on goon I just chilled out, drank a few beers and ate some BBQ food. If I am honest it was a bit boring. The campsites that we stayed at during our trip were extremely quiet, on night one there was only one other couple staying and they were a pair of fun sponges who just wanted to get an early night and maybe have some missionary.

The off-roading part of the trip was the main attraction and that is not as fun when you are sat in the back seat getting bumped around. There is no way my car would've been able to cope with the terrain of the island, but I would've loved to have ragged a rental 4x4 around it. Hindsight is a wonderful thing, at the time not driving and having a stress-free time seemed to be the best option, it also saved us a fair amount of money. That said, I wish that I had spent the extra $200 and went on a tour with some randoms, I am certain that would have resulted in a more fulfilling experience and another couple of mind-numbing hangovers.

Come the end of the trip I was very relaxed, full of nice food and feeling as fresh as I had in a long time, maybe a chilled couple of days was just what the doctor ordered. The calm was soon replaced with reality, as we got back to the mainland it became apparent that we only had seven days to get to Melbourne, just the 1000 miles away. I also had the small task of selling my beaten-up old Land Cruiser to a lucky buyer, it was time to get my ass in gear.

Monday 18th December 2017

Chevs and I bid farewell to ze Germans and made our way to the Sunshine Coast. On the way, I put my car up for sale on all of the websites and 4x4 pages I could find and prayed that someone wanted to pay me $4000 for Reginald II. I also sniffed out a mechanic nearby as one of the front lights wasn't working which made driving a night quite dangerous and very illegal. We jumped in a hostel and I drove Reg down to the mechanics. He was a lovely chap who said he would give the car a service for $50 after finding out I would be selling it soon, hopefully. I left the car in his capable hands for a couple of hours and Chevs and I popped to a local café for some lunch. I ordered a chicken pie and asked for it to not get heated up and the woman serving me nearly beat me up. 'You don't want your chicken pie heated up?' Her eyes were bulging out of her head like I had just asked if I could have some milk from her breasts. I prefer most foods cold.

With two hours wasted, I returned to the mechanic who didn't have the happiest of looks on his face. He didn't beat around the bush a jumped straight to his conclusion informing me that my truck was fucked. I tried to digest the news. 'Well of course it is, it's old and has 200,000 on the clock, I know it's not mint.' I replied knowing the car had seen better days. 'No mate, the car is proper fucked, it needs some serious work on it, probably four, five grand spent.' As the words came out of his mouth I nearly fell to the floor. Bollocks! There wasn't a chance in the world I was about to spend that sort of money on a car that I was only going to be driving for the next few days. Even if I wanted too I couldn't afford it, I had pissed most of my money up the wall down the coast. I stood expressionless in the garage for a few minutes trying to calculate the amount I had ballsed up. I am not good at maths but if my calculations were correct I had ballsed up catastrophically. I walked outside and got inside the money pit that was Reginald II, it was set to lose me about $3000 at this rate. I remained hopeful someone might buy it as a project so kept the adverts running for a few more days before potentially having to send it to the scrapyard in the sky.

The Sunshine Coast didn't have too much to offer for Chevs and me, we popped down to Brisbane but only for a quick dinner stop. We would've liked to have stayed a bit longer but we had to sell the car, get to Sydney and then on to Melbourne sharpish.

Tuesday 19th December 2017

The Gold Coast was a place that I didn't think a whole lot of. I saw the appeal and why it would have been a real hot spot for Australians to own properties, but it was just lots of fancy high-rises and skyscrapers along a nice beach. I tried to switch off to the fact that I was going to have a $3000-dollar Toyota Land Cruiser shaped hole in my bank balance and relaxed on the beach for the day. I struggled to relax, I was checking my messages and emails every other minute it was unbearable. At 3 pm with a cold ice-pole in hand, a message about the car finally popped into my inbox.

RE: Toyota Land Cruiser advert
Good Afternoon,
*Is this car still for sale? Looking for a cheap 4x4 project to do with my son and take him off-roading. Cash waiting. Call me on ************ and we can arrange.*
Thanks,
Harry's Saviour.

I called him immediately, he must've thought I was a bit keen and he would've been wrong, I was extremely keen! Please please please buy my car. He lived an hour away from Brisbane which wasn't too bad a drive at all considering Australia is a billion miles squared. I told him that I would drive the car to his house, but I couldn't afford a time-waster because I was due in Sydney that week. He understood and said he would pay for my petrol as a minimum if he didn't buy the car. I needed much more than petrol money but at this stage, he was the only person in the whole of Australia interested in my truck. Time to get into Wheeler Dealer mode, I needed to get this car out of my possession.

Wednesday 20th December 2017

It was a big day. I woke up feeling like I was about to play in the FA Cup Final, I had butterflies about selling the Land Cruiser. The drive up to the chaps house was tense, I was practising my sales pitches on

Chevs who was buying the car off of me every time to give me some confidence. We arrived in the middle of nowhere to the potential buyers' house and he came out to greet us at the bottom of his drive. He was very welcoming and loved the look of the car. He informed me that he was looking for a blank canvas to make his own which, in fairness, Reginald II was. He poked and prodded around the car for a few minutes, he knew enough about cars to realise that mine needed a bit of work doing but nothing fell off. I hoped he didn't know too much. He would mention something to me that I had no idea about and I would just agree to which he would respond 'I can sort that.'

'The left-wing processor bolts are off, aren't they?'

'Yeah, they still work but might need replacing.'

'I can sort that.'

He then asked the dreaded question that I knew was coming but prayed he'd just forget somehow, 'Can I take it for a quick drive?' Of course, I let him and handed over the keys with everything crossed that it started, moved and behaved for the next 20 minutes. It did, this bloke didn't mind this car at all you know, had I struck gold?

'So you want $4000 for it, yes?' Negotiations were underway, this was what I had been training for over the last day or so, hopefully, he was as easily persuaded as Chevs.

'I think $4000 is a fair price, it's a lot of car for the money, it has served me well, never missed a beat.' A white lie, it had missed a few beats.

'I'm thinking more $3000, it needs a fair bit of work but nothing that I can't do here.' $3000 was a more than fair price but I felt that if I just shook his hand then and there, he might wonder why I was so eager and have an extra check.

'$3000 is too low for me, I could probably drop $250 and meet you at $3750.' A firm backhand return, the ball was in his court. Let's skip the foreplay, all he had to do was offer me $3500 and I was ready to shake his hand off and run to Brisbane Airport.

'How about we meet somewhere in the middle, say $3500?' Inside I was screaming with joy, but I somehow remained calm on the surface.

'Cash?' He nodded in reply. 'You've got yourself a deal.' We shook hands and I turned to Chevs with pure relief and elation on my face. I had sold the Land Cruiser to a chap that was going to restore it to its former glory whilst spending a lot more money on it that he anticipated. He handed me the money and we signed the relevant documents, sale complete, what a day! Did I feel slightly bad that I had just sold a car that was quite crap? Yes. Would I do it again? Absolutely! The only problem was the fact that we were still an hour away from Brisbane Airport and that was where we needed to be to catch a flight to Sydney. I asked the chap who had just purchased my car if he knew any good local taxi companies to which he told me he was more than happy to take us to the airport. What a genuinely nice man I had just ripped off. Thankfully he was going to take us in his car which worked and had air-conditioning. What a gentleman.

We hopped in and he drove us to Brisbane airport, dropping us off like a family member would. I ensured not to talk about the car he had just bought on the journey as I didn't want him realising that I had no idea what I had just sold him. We jumped out of his car, thanked him and he drove off into the distance. I embraced Chevs as if I had just won the jackpot on the pokies, I basically had, what a stroke of luck.

Thursday 21st December 2019

We finally arrived in Sydney which was now Chevs's temporary home. There was also a little surprise at his flat in the shape of Callum Tyrie, the Judas who left us back in Cambodia. Tyrie had travelled and ended up in Australia with his now ex-girlfriend who had sacked him off whilst doing their farm work.. Hate to say I told you so Tyrie but I told you so. Chevs's flat was decent enough, it had two bedrooms, a Mario Balcony overlooking more flats and a fridge full of beer. Of course, there was only one thing on the agenda for this reunion and that was hundreds if not thousands of beers.

We caught up on what had been a pretty mental year for all of us, none of our plans had worked and we all ended up in places that we would've never imagined when setting off way back in January. Tyrie had travelled, gone home, travelled again and ended up in Sydney with Chevs. Chevs had travelled, completed farm work and settled in Sydney and I had travelled, been sacked from a farm, lived in Weipa for a while and was now coming to the end of my travels. This was the worst thing for me, Chevs and Tyrie would be staying in Australia into 2018 and beyond whereas I would be buying a flight home pretty soon for some time in early January. The beers and the catch up was sensational, I had missed being the trio of idiots that initially set out on this trip of a lifetime.

Friday 22nd December 2017

Whilst I was in Sydney, I thought I had better do some of the touristy stuff as well as getting beery. The main attraction in Sydney is the Opera House, which is situated on the river, anyone you know who has visited Sydney will have a picture in front of this, it's a modern wonder of the world. Chevs and Tyrie being the locals that they were became my tour guides for the day as we explored the city.

The Sydney Opera House was a lot smaller than I expected. I am sure inside it is wonderful and if you enjoy the opera then you would probably get suitably aroused by the site of this strange building. For me, it was just another funny-shaped building that didn't stand out. Making matters worse, we stopped for a pint in the bar and it was so highly-priced I nearly couldn't afford my flight home. $11 for a schooner, disgraceful pricing, it was my round as well.

The street performer that we passed on the way home was a better attraction than the Opera House itself and all he was doing was throwing knives around and catching them in his mouth. Sydney as a place wasn't a slice of me, it was just another busy city full of men in suits rushing about. I have heard that Manly is a good place to visit whilst in Sydney and I didn't venture that way so maybe it was my fault for thinking it was a below-par place. To me, it was just hot London.

Sunday 24th December 2017

We were crap travellers right until our last journey, we stayed loyal to our crapness. Instead of catching a flight to Melbourne the day before and leaving ourselves with plenty of time to settle into our Airbnb, we decided to catch the overnight train, on Christmas Eve. How very festive of us. This would result in us arriving in Melbourne on Christmas Day at 8 am, hideous. Macey, Thomo and Doug from Solent drunk times were coming over for the festive period as well and they were also arriving on Christmas morning, this made more sense for them though as it reduced their flight price by about £200. The Christmas Eve night train was as bad as you would imagine, we tried our best to lift the spirits and have a beer at midnight, but my head wasn't in it. I slept well on that train and arrived in Melbourne fresh and raring for Jesus's Birthday celebrations.

Monday 25th December

Christmas Day in Australia is not like it is in the UK, we had not planned to have a roast dinner and stay in the house. We had planned to chuck our stuff in the house and get ourselves down to St Kilda beach for festive beers and a bbq. Not only was Macey, Thomo and Doug over, so was Ross, another university friend, and a load of his mates from Devon that I had met previously on a Southampton bar crawl. Christmas Day was going to get drunk.

We got down the beach for midday and it was already very busy, every traveller and local had the same idea on Christmas Day. The sun was shining, we had far too many beers and Ross had bought a cricket set along with him. It was different and I liked it. Santa hats on we played cricket for hours on end getting drunker with every innings. Big Chevs peaked too early and ended up having a little nap on the beach fielding at mid-wicket. As I looked up the beach everyone was doing the same as what we were, not a care in the world and not a present in site. Happy Birthday, Jesus. One thing I can remember is meeting a girl that I nicknamed smiler because her mouth was too big for her face and she was always smiling.

Getting back to the Airbnb that night was a real struggle. I had stayed on the beach with a few of the Devon lads who were staying in a hostel nowhere near where was staying in. I had no idea where this Airbnb was and no one was picking up their phone. I went back and forth on a tram for half an hour hoping that I would recognise something, but I didn't, I was lost. Macey eventually picked his phone up and I jumped in a very expensive taxi back to the house where everyone was wide awake and playing card games. 'Didn't fancy picking up your phones then lads?'

Tuesday 26th December 2017

For those people that aren't cricket fans, this will not appeal you to one bit. The Boxing Day Test match between Australia and England was something I had been looking forward to for months. Luckily the lads that were over from Devon all loved cricket and so did I. Chevs, Thomo, Tyrie, Doug and Macey didn't mind it but they all liked drinking beers so I was sure they would have a good day. It was another scorcher and Chevs and I dressed up as ladies which turned out to be an inspired decision as wearing a dress meant that a little breeze crept up my leg now and then, very welcome on this hot day because my gentleman's area was melting off. As much as I love cricket, I must admit that after four hours of watching a Test match I was bored. There is only so much blocking and occasional LBW shouts I can bear. Luckily beer kept us entertained, anything becomes more entertaining after a load of beers. This is a scientifically proven fact because I've watched University Challenge on the TV whilst drinking and it was quite funny. The Boxing Day Test was something ticked off of my bucket list so that's a positive and The Barmy Army were in full voice which was great to be a part of! I'm not sure how these men and woman manage to sneak off to Australia for a few months over Christmas to watch cricket, do they have no jobs?

28th December 2017

Melbourne was like one big reunion site for me over the festive period, I was half expecting to get a message from the annoying

Danish lads from Cambodia to see if I fancied a game of beer pong. Today was a day full of drinking and meeting up with a few people that were also in the area. The first port of call was meeting up with Harley who I hadn't seen since Hue. We had kept in touch and had his brother's best mate Doug with us this time around, so it was an even better occasion to get drunk. Harley had even more tattoos and was still the same carefree quizmaster that I had met back in Vietnam. I also met up with Asta and some of her friends finishing off a strong squad for an all-dayer.

The lads from Devon never turn down the chance to get on the beers so they joined us on our little Melbourne bar crawl adventure. Meeting up with Harley made me reminisce on Hue and Vietnam in general, god that was a good time to be alive! There were no ass-flavoured shots in Melbourne so we had to deal with the closest thing to it, tequila, which Asta was very happy with. It had only been a month since I had seen Asta so this wasn't so much a reunion it was more of a challenge to see how drunk we could get now we are out of Weipa not worrying about work tomorrow. The answer was convincingly very drunk, we popped into every pub and bar that was open. It was like being at home on a bar crawl, all my good mates were there and it got out of hand very quickly. Before I knew it I was in a bar with my shirt over my head rubbing my stomach against Doug's. The next bar we tried to enter rejected us which at the time resulted in an argument but did us a favour, we were all legless!

Amongst the madness we had also planned what we would be doing for New Year's Eve, Asta was going to a bar on the riverfront, which was a free bar with $75 entry, so not technically speaking a free bar, but reasonable enough for it to tempt me. Yes please and thank you. She did invite us, we weren't just going to crash it like the losers that we were. It took no time at all to convince everyone else that this was a good plan.

30th December 2017

We had a day of mooching around St Kilda and shopping for some cool clothes to wear for NYE. I had no suitable clothes in my rucksack, all my clothes were offensive and borderline revolting. St Kilda was a cool place and the longer I spent in it the more I liked it. Doug was getting the same feeling and I watched him get the travel bug right in front of my eyes. He asked me lots of questions about my adventures and I gave him the solid advice of don't use me as an example but travelling is very worth it. It is difficult to explain to someone why it is so good, of course, you have lots of freedom and the places that you visit are great but when I spoke about my travels it just sounded like a big party with some work wedged in between, as I am sure you will agree if you've made it this far.

I left Doug to make his own decision and we proceeded to purchase the waviest garms that St Kilda had to offer. I also purchased a hat because I thought it looked cool and it covered my dreadful blonde barnet. Better to look like a budget Indiana Jones than a receding Cruella de Vil.

31st December 2017

The party we had all been waiting for, NYE in Melbourne. The party we attended was very different, it had a strict number of guests which meant it wasn't rammed and it was, dare I say, quite classy. Everyone put on their best clothes and we didn't look too out of place at this party despite some questionable shirts and me wearing an Indiana Jones inspired hat.

The class was soon taken out of the occasion once everyone had spent a couple of hours drinking free rum and vodka. The dance floor was full of men with their ties around their heads and women slut dropping in their dinner dresses. The Australians know how to get loose, what can I say. We needed no excuse to get our money's worth and tried our very best to drink this lovely bar dry. It was the perfect setting to see the New Year in. During the night I was dancing with a lady who took my hat off revealing my flattened black and blonde balding shit lid. She told me that she wasn't expecting that and put it back on, a real confidence booster.

HAPPY NEW YEARS!! Fireworks went off on the river and I embraced those around me. I had tried and failed throughout the night to find a suitable young lady to kiss at the start of 2018 so ended up kissing Tyrie and accepting 2018 wasn't about to be my year. Ross Abraham once famously quoted whilst on the way back from a university night out in Bournemouth on the 6 am morning train 'It doesn't get better than this!' He is a modern-day Martin Luther King. Up until that moment in Melbourne he had been right. University had been the pinnacle of my life and I had loved every second. But now university had to accept defeat and sit in second place as travelling had overtaken it as the peak of my life. As I stood on the side of the river in Melbourne with my best mates, drunk as could be, I told Ross 'It doesn't get better than this.' And he agreed. We had peaked. I had peaked. My life had been so carefree over the last year and I knew that the New Year and most years that followed just wouldn't compare.

Bloody hell that was a bit reflective, you'll be glad to know that we all ended up in Melbourne Casino that night and got stupendously shit-faced and lost $100 on red trying to pay for my plane ticket. I woke up on one sofa with Chevs completely naked on the other with a blanket covering most of him, just not his balls they were very much out! There is nothing I would have rather woke up too on my last day of travelling.

Tuesday 2nd January 2018
So that's that, just shy of a year of travelling done, dusted and documented. I had seen ping pong shows, ladyboys and even killed a puppy on my birthday. I had spent 75% of my money on alcohol and the rest I just wasted. All I had to do was endure the 24-hour flight home back to the surprisingly bearable and very cold UK, no crying babies and not a pisshead insight. The peace allowed me time to reflect which I did whilst smiling from ear-to-ear. With a stupidly expensive gin and tonic in hand I wrote down my last few thoughts and closed the book and that chapter of my life. I had travelled to Hanoi, Bangkok and Koh Rong and Pattaya over the last year, but my final destination was Yeovil via Mumbai and Bristol Airport.

The Aftermath

When I returned home, everything was the same as I left it, my friends asked me a couple of times about my travels and then it was all quickly forgotten about. No one gave a shit about the elephants that I saw in Chiang Mai or how amazing Halong Bay was and rightfully so. I surprised my mum by coming home a week earlier than she expected which was a nice surprise for her, dad wasn't so impressed with my early return, I would be straight back at the table for a roast dinner and a couple of his Yorkshire puddings. I was more surprised than they were on returning home as my mum had given away my Ford Fiesta to my auntie and my dad had donated my TV to the local cricket club, excellent. It was lovely to see the rest of my family over the coming weeks, they were slightly more interested in my stories than my friends were but even they got bored with them eventually. It was also great to see my two dogs Boris and Bert who thankfully hadn't forgotten about me. I never told them that I had run over one of their kind in Vietnam. Wolfy, my best mate, was delighted about my return and I was so happy to see him. We went straight to the local pub and drank bottles of cheap wine. We did this every Wednesday for about two months on my return, we had a lot of catching up to do! I gave the occasional bit of advice to those who were travelling themselves, but the sad thing was it was all now a memory and their travelling plans just made me incredibly jealous. Doug went off on his adventure to South East Asia with his girlfriend and every Instagram post was like a nudge for me to go again but it never happened.

For a short while, I debated travelling to South America but that would've been a trip that I would have to complete on my own, I wasn't up for that, sounds scary. So, I did what everyone else does, I got a job and I started my very normal and relatively boring life which I don't mind at all. At least I'm not picking avocados in Tolga.

I hope you have enjoyed reading about my travels as much as I enjoyed participating in them. If I have come across as 'rah, travelled yah' please let me know and I will proceed to walk onto the M5.

For now, I'm going to continue to avoid adulthood as often as humanly possible. I hope you do too.

Printed in Great Britain
by Amazon

50752325R00095